A SOLDIER'S
FAITH

A SOLDIER'S FAITH

SPIRITUAL LESSONS FROM THE BATTLEFIELD

JOHN LOVING

ANOMALOS PUBLISHING HOUSE
CRANE

Anomalos Publishing House, Crane 65633
© 2008 by John Loving
All rights reserved. Published 2008
Printed in the United States of America
08   1
ISBN-10: 0981509169 (paper)
EAN-13: 9780981509167 (paper)

Cover illustration and design by Steve Warner

All Bible quotations are from the New International Version.

A CIP catalog record for this book is available from the Library of
Congress.

To my children and grandchildren,
so that they might read this and believe.

Contents

Foreword

A *Soldier's Faith* will place you in the middle of the attack. You will sense the fear of being on the front line, and you will be challenged to consider how faith is involved in war. John Loving, in this personal story about his own discoveries during his journey as a soldier in Vietnam, opens our hearts and minds to give credence to the possibility that a loving God can actually use war to cause us to draw near to Him even in the midst of all the turmoil, fears, and death found in combat.

Could it be possible that for some of us it's only in the middle of a crisis or the battles of life and death, such as war, that we are willing to consider whether God is real? You might just realize, as Loving did in battle, that we can actually discover peace while in the process of waging our daily individual battles or even in the midst of the horror of wars created by men.

This is a compelling story of providence, provision, and protection as understood through the eyes of faith. John's insight into character, leadership, and faith applies to each of us and can be adapted to all aspects of life, whether you are a soldier, a business-person, or a professional in the marketplace.

A Soldier's Faith touched me as a real-life story challenging me to consider the meaning and purpose for my life. I hope that you also expand your search to understand the giver of faith and that, like the author, you will find purpose in the struggles, together with the faith in the one who uses these struggles for our good and His glory.

Patrick A. O'Neal
CBMC, Inc., National Executive Director
Chatham Development Corporation, President

Preface

Approximately ten years ago I began writing an account of my experiences as a U.S. Army first lieutenant, serving as a combat advisor in Vietnam. In the beginning my primary purpose in writing was to pass on to my children and grandchildren a record of the events I had experienced during the war, but as the work progressed the book expanded, and the final result was *Combat Advisor: How America Won the War and Lost The Peace In Vietnam.* That book related many personal experiences that had formed my view of the Vietnam War, and how that war has affected the U.S. Military and the American people. While relating these events, I also became aware of how many of them had influenced the development of my character as a young man and my faith as a Christian.

At that time, I found myself wanting to explore these experiences further from a faith viewpoint, and relate how they had sometimes challenged and at other times affirmed my core beliefs and values. Since *Combat Advisor*, by its nature, had a more secular purpose, I resolved to reexamine someday the record with a view to diving more deeply into these issues of faith and morality and extracting from them principles that have value from a Christian point of view.

The result is this book. I am neither a theologian nor a trained pastor, and my only authority for attempting this writing is that God seems to have led me to the undertaking and then led me through the process. I am merely a testifier to the work that I saw God do in that troubled land during those troubled times. This endeavor has further caused me to recognize sin in my own life, to seek to repent, and to receive redemption, a process that continues to this day.

I hope and pray that *A Soldier's Faith* will provide spiritual inspiration to young and older readers alike, but I especially pray that it will be of use to young people, so many of whom seem to have decided that religion, especially organized religion, is not relevant to their modern lives. While writing this book, I prayerfully considered those young men and women who are either serving in the military or contemplating military service. They, more than any of their contemporaries, face moral issues and dilemmas of conscience that are not being satisfactorily resolved in the secular world. If this writing finds its way into the hands of only a few of those young warriors, and proves to be useful to them, then I will finally know why I was spared when so many others around me were killed or grievously wounded in the Vietnam War.

Acknowledgements

I need to thank several people who helped make this book a reality. I wish to thank my wife Lennis who endured the process and suggested several improvements to the text. Next, I wish to thank Reverend Keith Glover who read my manuscript and checked to be sure that, in his words, I "did not say anything that is heretical." My fellow warriors for Christ at the Triangle Chapter of CBMC (Christian Businessmen's Connection) have given me valuable support and encouragement.

I must also thank Command Sergeant Major Mack Rice (U.S. Army Ret.) for allowing me to tell his story and Lieutenant Colonel Lloyd Stark (U.S. Army Ret.) for remembering after almost forty years and for encouraging me in ways he may not even realize. Finally, I need to thank my parents, the late Charles and Gladys Loving, for passing on to me their love of the Lord and his Church.

ONE

Surrender

Submit yourselves to God.
Resist the devil, and he will flee from you.
—JAMES 4:7

I went to Vietnam in the spring of 1969 to serve as a combat advisor with South Vietnamese Regional Forces in Tay Ninh Province. At that time I was an infantry first lieutenant and had received extensive training in infantry weapons and tactics, as well as instruction in the Vietnamese culture and language. I was only twenty-three years old, but had already served in a difficult stateside command position, and felt very capable of carrying out the mission I had been assigned. Little did I know as I assumed command of my six man advisory team, that before my mission was completed my competency as a leader and my faith as a Christian would be severely tested.

Throughout that spring and summer of 1969 I encountered many situations that would tax my ability to perform as a professional soldier and also test my ability to deal tactfully and diplomatically with my Vietnamese counterparts. At my first duty station in the small village of Ben Cau, I came under fire from the enemy almost immediately, surviving attacks from two snipers as well as numerous mortar barrages that were uncannily timed so as to catch my men and me in the open with no cover. As summer came to an end my team was transferred to another village, Tra Vo, which was less remote and located on the banks of the Vam Co Duong River. From this village my team operated with RF (Regional Force) Company 766 and other South Vietnamese units in operations that were designed to stop the flow of enemy soldiers and materials along and across the river.

In the beginning, one of the tactics employed by my superiors was to place a platoon of South Vietnamese soldiers and two American advisors in large landing craft that would ply up and down the river all night, enticing the VC (Viet Cong) to shoot at the boat, which they did quite often. If the boat came under fire, then the platoon would be ordered to disembark and attack the enemy. Our first attempt was largely successful. After several hours of motoring up and down the river, the enemy fired a rocket at our ship, hitting the upper port rail and exploding harmlessly in the air. As planned, I answered the attack with artillery and then ordered my men to disembark and attack the enemy on shore. There were some tense moments at first when our men who were supposed to lead the attack remained frozen standing in the open door of the craft, presenting easy targets to the VC. Luckily we were not fired upon, and the Vietnamese lieutenant launched the attack by unceremoniously grabbing some of our men by the seat of the pants and tossing them off the boat. The subsequent attack by our troops resulted in the capture of a RPG (Rocket Propelled Grenade Launcher) and three rockets. I surmised that we must have killed or wounded one or more of the enemy, who were dragged off leaving this weapon and ammunition behind.

A NEW STRATEGY

Unfortunately, after several weeks of subsequently less successful attempts at this type of operation, it became obvious that we were probably experiencing more casualties on our side than we were causing among the enemy. The day after our first successful attack, I received a report over the radio that three sailors were killed when one of them dropped one of the rockets that we had captured. The report said that they had been "playing with them" on the dock where we had left them the night before.

Later, during another operation the enemy attacked one of our boats killing the pilot, a young ensign I knew, and severely wounding a first lieutenant and a staff sergeant from our district headquarters. A week after that incident, a PT boat packed with South Vietnamese soldiers was attacked with rockets and small arms and we lost nine men who were killed or wounded. It became obvious that a new strategy was required.

The new strategy that came down to us from headquarters still involved taking platoons of soldiers out in boats at night, but the new twist was to drop them in strategically picked locations to set up ambushes. Once this strategy was underway, I must admit that I felt considerably better waiting in ambush for the enemy on land than I had felt floating up and down the river in what was starting to resemble a large steel coffin.

RF Company 766, which was stationed with us at Tra Vo, was selected to go on the first ambush. On a dark night in the middle of August, I walked down our company street with my senior NCO, Sergeant Melvin Davis, and our Vietnamese interpreter, Sergeant Nea, to the Tra Vo dock on the east side of the Van Co Dom River. A platoon from the 766 met us there where we boarded a large landing craft and headed up river to a pre-selected site where the enemy was reported to have been active.

We unloaded at the prescribed location at about 2000 hours and set up our ambush. The Vietnamese lieutenant, who was the platoon leader, was an officer I had come to know well and was one that I respected for his ability. He positioned his men in a tree line along a stream that ran next to a large rice paddy, and then put his headquarters element on a bare spot of ground next to the river. I felt that the ambush formation was good since the enemy was expected to come down the stream headed for the river and the bulk of his men should be able to engage them at the stream.

As Dave, Nea, and I sat down at the HQ site, Nea wisely asked what would we do if we came under attack since there was no cover immediately available. Without giving it much thought, I responded that we would slide over the edge of the bank of the river where we would be protected and could return fire. I should have checked out the bank to be sure it was suitable for this purpose, but I did not. I knew that in most places along the river, the bank dropped down a couple of feet to the shore where there would be some firm ground with the river gradually filling up the space behind.

Sgt. Davis and I sat back-to-back watching in different directions, while Thieu uy, Vietnamese for Second Lieutenant, moved back and forth between his men and our position. As a rule, I never slept on these ambushes. The night was not only dark but also very quiet, with no sounds other than the continuous sounds of frogs and insects singing. Suddenly the silence was broken with the roar of machine gun fire, and I saw red tracers cutting across the landscape in front of us. Per my ill-conceived plan, I lay down and rolled over the edge of the riverbank. To my great surprise, instead of landing on firm ground below, I went into water over my head. As I resurfaced, trying to hold my rifle out of the water, I saw Nea flying over my head landing in the water behind me, and Dave plunging in at my right side. We were all splashing around in the water when Thieu uy peered over the edge of the bank and exclaimed in an excited voice, "No VC, no VC, boat, US boat." Quickly, he reached out, grabbed my hand and pulled me out. I immediately pulled out Dave who pulled out Nea.

We then all ran toward a rice paddy dike about 50 meters away, with bullets kicking up the dirt around our feet and red tracers whizzing past our heads. As we ran, I pieced together what was happening. A U.S. Navy boat, a landing craft similar to the one that had dropped us off, was out in the water just below where the stream entered the river, and its machine gunner was firing a 50-

caliber machine gun through our ambush position. At this point I could not imagine why a Navy boat should be firing at us, but I would learn later that the enemy had come in undetected to the edge of the river just below the stream and fired a rocket at the boat as it moved up the river. Naturally the machine gunner on the boat returned fire and continued to fire.

Miraculously, the lieutenant, Dave, Nea, and I all reached the dike without being hit. As we settled down behind the small dike, which was only about one foot thick and one foot high, I recalled that a 50-caliber machine gun is a very large gun that fires a bullet that is about the size of a large man's thumb. It is the most powerful gun in the U.S. Army's small arms arsenal, can penetrate most unarmored metals, and would easily tear through the dike once the boat arrived in front of our position.

The rice paddy was void of rice plants at that time but was covered with a thin layer of water and was very muddy. As I lay there, with the loud thumping of the huge gun ringing in my ears, I tried to clear my mind enough to decipher what we could do to get out of this predicament. The gunner was now spraying the entire countryside around us and the bullets were either coursing over our heads or plowing up the ground in front of us with each pass. I reasoned that within another minute or two the boat would be directly in front of our position where the gun would begin to do the most damage. We couldn't get up and run because there was enough visibility that the gunner would probably be able to see us and mow us down. I decided that we must stay where we were and hope for the best.

A TIME FOR PRAYER

Without really thinking about it I began to pray. I prayed the only prayer I knew, the Lord's Prayer. "Our father who art in Heaven," I recited to myself. Then a thought came to me. I remembered that I was carrying a small hand held strobe light that would produce a bright blinking light when activated. If I turned it on and held it up high, I reasoned, perhaps the gunner would see it and stop firing, realizing that I was an American since the VC were not likely to have such a device. I was reaching for it in my pocket when a picture flashed into my mind. I seemed to be transported in my imagination to the boat where I was standing behind the gunner who was leaning into his terrible weapon firing long bursts of rounds into the shoreline. In this vision, I saw my strobe begin to blink to his right, and it looked like the muzzle flash of a rifle firing. The gunner instinctively turned the machine gun to the right and fired into the blinking light. I decided to leave the strobe in my pocket.

At that point I perceived that the only thing that I could do was try to protect myself, and since my head was my most vulnerable spot, I frantically began to dig a small hole in the mud with my bare hands, and put my head into it propping my helmet up in front. Then I began to pray again, holding my breath because the hole immediately filled with water. I started over with, "Our father who art in heaven, hallowed be thy name, thy kingdom come, thy will be done...." Suddenly I realized that was the answer. My will didn't matter anymore. I had done all that I could do and there was nothing more for me to try. I had to surrender my will to God.

I lifted my head and looked to the right at the line of men lying next to me in the mud. First there was Dave, and then Nea, and then the Vietnamese lieutenant and about fifteen of his men. Dave and Nea were my direct responsibility. The Vietnamese also looked to me for leadership. It was my responsibility to take care of them, and to show them the right thing to do. Now they were all in jeopardy of being killed, and there was nothing I could do for them. So I muttered beneath the defining noise of the gun, "Lord, there is nothing I can do to save these men or myself. I turn it over to you. Your will be done."

I put my head back into the hole I had dug and waited for the seemingly inevitable crashing sound of those large bullets smashing into the small dike in front of us. As the boat slowly plowed its way to where it was almost perpendicular with our position, the gun abruptly ceased singing its terrible song, and there was silence that seemed as loud as the gun had seemed. I heard only the drone of the diesel engines that powered the boat. I carefully raised my head until I could see the gray hulk of the large craft slowly moving up the river.

THE POWER OF SURRENDER

That was the first time that I had surrendered my will to God, and had asked him to take a burden of mine and do with it as he willed. Since then I have done it many times whenever I have been troubled by some problem or impending danger. Also, since that day the Lord's Prayer has become my constant companion and I repeat it at least daily.

Some people would say that this is a story of answered prayer. Of course that could be said, and it certainly was prayer answered. However, I think of it more as a case of surrendered will into the loving hands of God, rather than an answer to prayer. I did not say to God "save me." Rather I said, "your will be done," and that is a different thing entirely. When we pray, we tend to ask for things we want. We may ask for material things, and I am reminded of the humorous Janis Joplin song that was played on the radio in the 1980's, that asked, "O Lord, won't you buy me a Mercedes Benz?"[1] There is nothing wrong with this because the Lord wants us to have the things we need, although that may not include a Mercedes Benz. Additionally, we may also pray other more selfless prayers for other people, for those who are sick or bereft, for our nation, or for some worthy cause such as world peace. In each case we are asking God to do something we have decided we want because it is good for us or somebody else.

I am not saying that we should not pray for those things. Prayer is by necessity a very important part of a Christian's life, and we should always pray for what we know in our hearts is right and good. We must pray, and pray often, because that is how we have a relationship with our Father. I am suggesting that when we pray for those things we want that we believe to be worthy, we should also say, "Lord your will be done, not mine," because we do not always know what is best, even though we think we do. Have you ever wanted something badly and not received it, and later, maybe years later, discovered that you really did not need it or that you are actually better off with out it? There is an old Chinese curse that says in essence, "May all your prayers be answered."

The Bible says, "Submit yourselves, then, to God. Resist the devil, and he will flee from you" (James 4:7). It may be possible sometimes that what we think we want is actually inspired by forces that are not good. At these times we may want a thing for less than admirable reasons. The first line of the old song mentioned above elaborates to say, "O Lord won't you buy me a Mercedes Benz? My friends all drive Porches, I must make amends." Sometimes we are driven by motives, possibly unrecognized motives, such as pride or greed, and it is always best whenever this is a possibility to say, "God's will be done, not mine."

Surrendering to God can be a powerful tool. When something difficult, perhaps seemingly impossible, has to be accomplished, who better to put in charge than The Lord? This is not to say we should do nothing ourselves to accomplish the task. We must do all that we can, and if the task is truly important, summon every bit of our energy, use every bit of our skill, and expend all of our resources to accomplish the job. But all along the way we must pray for God's assistance and then turn the outcome over to him.

In his inspiring and much read book, *Experiencing God*, Henry Blackaby explains that God wants us to join him in his work, and when we take up the challenge to do his will to the best of our ability then it becomes God's responsibility, not ours, to make the outcome successful.[2] That is a powerful and reassuring thought, that if we do all that we can do, then the Lord will take over, and if it is his will our success is assured. Likewise, we can rest in the thought that if it is not his will, we are not responsible for the outcome. If the outcome is successful, however, we must remember to give the credit to God and not take it for ourselves. Moses was the Lord's good and faithful servant, but when the Israelites were complaining of the lack of water in the desert, he lifted his staff and struck a rock saying, "… must we bring you water out of this rock?" God brought forth water from the rock, but Moses had made the mistake of saying "we" when it was God alone who brought water from the rock. As a result, Moses was not allowed to enter the Promised Land at the end of the Israelites' long and difficult journey.

MORAL AND SPIRITUAL QUESTIONS

My experience in the rice paddy that night changed the way I felt and thought about my religion. I began to view God as a real and powerful entity who cared about me and was active in the world, and I began to think of Jesus Christ as my Lord and Savior. In his book *Tender Warrior*, Stu Weber describes "wake-up calls" that he received as he matured as a Christian.[3] He says that one occurred in Vietnam in a muddy ditch. I received a "wake-up call" that night while lying face down in a muddy rice paddy. It was the first of three that I would receive before I left Vietnam. Additionally I began to consider certain questions about my faith and spirituality. I was facing what Henry Blackaby calls a "crisis of belief." Blackaby uses the term in his book *Experiencing God*, to refer to doubts that nearly always arise when Christians decide to pursue what they believe to be the will of God.[4] For me this "crisis of belief" occurred because my faith had never been grounded, and when I needed most to know what I *really* believed, I did not know.

Two Godly people, my parents, had raised me in the Church, and at the age of twelve I had made a decision to accept Christ as my savior. The early Christian training I had received was still in the back of my mind and was being pushed forward by the maturing experience of war. Solomon says in Proverbs, "Hear, my son, your father's instruction and reject not your mother's teaching" (Prov. 1:8). I had been born a Christian and raised a Christian, but my faith had never been tested, and I suddenly did not know what I really believed. Now I was a twenty-three-year-old man who was on my own and experiencing what would probably be the greatest challenge of my entire life. I had to decide in what did I believe and where did my salvation reside? Was it in this earthly life, where I must rely only on my own competence, or was it in a Higher Being where I could find strength in times of trouble, and where I could find salvation if my competence proved to be insufficient?

During the weeks and months that followed, I would continue to ponder this question, and others would also arise. Because the war was so intense, and I had to stay focused on doing my duty and at the same time staying alive, I resisted thinking too much on these things. nevertheless, the war became a time of decision for me, and I had to decide on the moral standards that I would live by. Would I conform to the standards of the world and worldly values, or would I live by the Christian standards that my parents had taught me? This book is about my struggle to answer those questions, a struggle that continues to this day. Only now, almost thirty-nine years later, do I see some of the things that God was doing then and trying to show me then.

The questions were not new. Some had sat unanswered in the back of my mind for some time. The questions that struggled to emerge from my subconscious then, and remained with me for years after I returned home, were these:

- Is there a God, and if there is a God, does he care what happens to me here on earth?
- Is it moral for a soldier to kill other human beings in wartime?
- If the answer to the above question is yes, must the war be a "just war," and if so, what is a truly "just war?"
- What is courage?
- Is there a Devil?
- What standards should a Christian live by?
- What is required of a Christian leader?

The war caused me to consider these things because it forced me to recognize that I am mortal. It has been said that those who experience war are aged beyond their years. People say that you can see it in the eyes of those who have known combat, a sad but knowing look that is unmistakable. Some say that it comes from the ordeal of struggling to stay alive, the fatigue of battle, or the psychological trauma of being under fire. I say that it is the result of being too close to death, and having to admit that maybe we are not invincible. Call it a loss of innocence if you like, but ultimately it is the sudden realization that we are mortal.

In the Bible, Job laments, "Man born of woman is of few days and full of trouble. He springs up like a flower and withers away. Like a fleeing shadow, he does not endure" (Job 14:1, 2). Like Job, we must first realize, that we are mortal, that life by any measure is short compared to the length of eternity, and that if we are to have any hope, we must put our faith into a power greater than ourselves; for if we must rely only on our own competence, our own self-sufficiency, we will have to eventually fail. In subsequent chapters we will look at my other two "wake-up calls" and explore these questions, but first let's consider our warrior heritage as Americans.

TWO

Our Warrior Heritage

You will hear of wars and rumors of wars...

—Matthew 24:6

Since the war for American Independence of 1775, each successive generation of Americans has had its wars to fight. The American people have grown accustomed to sending their young people off to war, and the progression of military conflicts has been relentless.

The American Revolution was soon followed by the war of 1812, and shortly after that came the war with Mexico. The Civil War then followed in the 1860s, and was a pivotal point in our history of conflicts that not only tore apart the Nation but tore apart families as well. The number of Americans who died in this tragic pitting of brother against brother exceeds the number of Americans who have died in all our other wars combined.

Following the Civil War there was a period of relative calm interrupted only by the short-lived Spanish American War. Then came the turn of the century and war clouds began to gather over Europe as the German Kaiser marshaled his forces for the start of World War I. America entered the fray in 1914 on the side of Britain and France, saving those countries from certain annihilation. The victorious allies then saddled Germany with huge reparation payments which, combined with the depression of the early 1930s, left the Germans destitute and discouraged, making the stage ready for the entrance of Hitler and his Third Reich. This led to World War II, and in 1942 American troops had to cross the Atlantic again to help the Brits put down the Hun menace.

After only a short respite, World War II was followed in the early 1950s by the Korean Conflict, which was initially not called a war because it was labeled a police action, initiated by the United Nations to preserve "world peace and order." The men who fought there and the families of the 54,000 who died there, have since rightly opted for the label "Korean War."

When I was in the fourth grade, my teacher, Mr. Wells, a retired U.S. Navy commander, gave us a brief rundown of these wars in our history class. After he recounted the list, he looked around the room, and then it seemed that his eyes rested on me when he said, "You boys in the room need to understand that each generation has had its war, and yours is likely to be no different. You might as well get used to the idea that you will probably have to fight someday just as your fathers and grandfathers had to fight."

Mr. Wells was right, and by the time I graduated from high school, Vietnam was already on the radar screen as the military conflict that would soon occupy the attention of my generation. After graduating from college with an ROTC commission as a second lieutenant, I entered the United States Army in April 1968 and began training to be an infantry officer in Vietnam.

Since the Vietnam War, our national leaders have managed to involve our country in other conflicts that have continued the tradition of thrusting our young men, and now young women, into harm's way. There was Desert Storm in Iraq in 1991, and then Afghanistan in 2001, and then the invasion of Iraq in 2003. Since the terrorist attacks on September 11, 2001, we have been prosecuting what the U.S. Government calls the "War on Terrorism," which seems to have the potential for offering endless opportunities for further involvement in military conflicts.

WHY SO MANY WARS?

Why should the United States, with its stated national goals of living in peace and prosperity with universal freedom for all, be beset throughout its history with so many wars and military conflicts? The answer is not easily forthcoming. Each war has had its own distinct origins and characteristics, and we can find specific reasons that are given for its justification in each instance. As a general statement, the traditional, and probably still the best, answer is that freedom is not free, and must be constantly defended. This is not to say that our leaders have always made the best decisions when thrusting us into these periods of combat, but it does say that this desire to protect freedom and our way of life against all comers may have made us more susceptible to perceived threats, whether real or imagined. It may be that our freedom is so dear, and the alternative to freedom so abhorrent, that our desire to protect it, like a she wolf protecting her cubs, has at times clouded our judgment and inspired a rush to war.

The purpose of this discourse is to merely point to the fact that throughout the history of our country, wars have been seemingly inevitable, and our warrior heritage is deeply ingrained in our psyche. The justification for war, or the lack of justification, will be discussed later in chapter 3. The point here is that war, and the need for citizen soldiers, has been a repeating occurrence in our history and is apparently an inevitable part of our future. As Winston Churchill said, "The story of the human race is war. Except for brief and precarious interludes there has never been peace in the world."

Just as war has been an important part of our history, so has religion played an important role in the conduct of those wars. Our leaders have often invoked the power of God when we have undertaken theses struggles. The Civil War was probably the most notable example, when the Generals on both sides sought to invoke the power of The Almighty to help them prevail against their enemies on the eve of battle. One of General Andrew Jackson's most trusted senior staff members was his chaplain, and he is said to have kept this officer close by at all times. Abraham Lincoln was apparently aware of this paradox of competing prayers for victory. At a meeting in the White House, he was asked by a supporter to pray that God would be with them in their efforts to win the war. He responded that he would not, but that he would pray that *they* would be with God as *he* pursued *his* objectives.

THE ROLE OF CHAPLAINS

An indication of the importance of religion in wartime has been the crucial role played by American military chaplains since the founding of our nation. In 1775 The Continental Congress authorized the recruiting of chaplains to accompany the Continental Army at a pay of twenty dollars per month. The founding fathers considered this function to be so important that the pay was elevated the very next year to thirty-three dollars and thirty-three cents per month.

This high regard for parsons in uniform continued as an important part of America's military during the early 1800s and into the Civil War period when they were highly valued and found in large numbers on both sides of the conflict. Each side, as mentioned before, felt obliged to summon Divine calamity on the other, but there were also reports of great revivals being held where thousands of tough fighting men publicly recounted their sins and surrendered their souls to God.

The value of the Chaplaincy was also shown in World War I when stories were told of bravery on the battlefield and at sea by men of the cloth who administered spiritual comfort to soldiers, marines, and sailors under fire. Likewise, chaplains were highly valued in World War II and lauded for their bravery and their devotion to the fighting men in their units. During World War II there were almost 10,000 chaplains in military service (approximately one for every 1,200 soldiers), and numerous chapels were erected for them all over the world.

As we approached modern times, the importance of chaplains in the military began to decline. During the Korean War their total number amounted to only 1,448, approximately one for every 4,000 soldiers. Vietnam brought on an era of new lows for the Chaplaincy Corps in both numbers and influence among our fighting men, a sad situation that certainly contributed to the decline in moral values as well as the decline in morale among our fighting men that occurred during that tragic war. In his book *The Faith of the American Soldier*, Stephen Mansfield states that "When many denominations in the United States lost faith in the American cause in Vietnam, they stopped sending chaplains, exacerbating the moral and spiritual crisis among the troops. Drugs, racial tension, the lack of a moral rationale for the war, and the seeming unwillingness on the part of the nation's leaders to fight so as to win—all made the chaplain's challenge in Vietnam an overwhelming task."[1]

My own experience in Vietnam supported this observation. Since I was a combat advisor located in remote parts of South Vietnam, my exposure to chaplains was very limited. I remember seeing a chaplain outside of a chapel only once. A tall American captain wearing a cross on his lapel stepped out of the supply helicopter one morning and announced that he would like to talk with my men about God. I welcomed him warmly, and we all gathered around to hear what he had to say. His talk was short but inspiring, and served to remind me that we were still human beings, and that God loved us. He gave us each a small paperback Bible and a small plastic cross that glowed in the dark. I still have that cross, and it is one of my most prized possessions.

It seems that today the Chaplain's Corps is faring better than it did during the Vietnam era, but there are still problems that result from military policies that prohibit chaplains from getting anywhere near the fighting and discourages entering into any discussions of faith that might prove to be controversial. Reporting on interviews he conducted with soldiers and chaplains in Iraq, Mansfield quotes one chaplain as saying, "Most of us want to talk about the things soldiers need to discuss: Is this war just? Is God on our side? Is killing in this war moral?" Regarding the prohibition against getting near the fighting, the same chaplain stated, "I want to serve fighting men and women while they fight. I don't want to make the sign of the cross from a safe distance. Something's got to change."

Mansfield visited Iraq in 2004, and the primary conclusion that he seems to have reached from his visit is that there is a strong expression of faith among our young people serving in combat and a strong desire on their part to study and learn moral and religious lessons as well as seek the comfort that comes from a firm belief in God and his faithful plan for our lives. This is good news indeed, and should be celebrated and encouraged whenever possible.

NO ATHEISTS IN FOXHOLES

As a nation, our warrior heritage has been a recurring thread in our historical record. Likewise, our reliance on a belief in God has been a recurring theme during these times of distress and conflict. My own experience has been that throughout my life my ability to cope with difficult challenges, fears, and temptations has been directly tied to my ability to remember my faith in God and the moral principals I learned as a child. My service during the Vietnam War was the most intense time of my life, and a time when I had to rely most upon my belief in a higher being. In my earlier book, *Combat Advisor*, I talked about military lessons learned from the Vietnam War that have relevance to modern wars.[2] Today, as I recall lessons of faith, morality, and character development that many soldiers have leaned during the extraordinary experience of war, I feel that they are not only relevant now, but that they are timeless principles for living a meaningful life.

Does it take an experience such as war to awaken a person's faith? Certainly not, but for some of us, life-threatening, or life-changing experiences do give us extra insight into the real meaning of our lives, and cause us to ask healthy questions about our purposes for living. It has been said that there are no atheists in foxholes. This is not true for everyone, and I must say that I have known exceptions, but in my case the experience of war was a deciding factor in my choosing to follow Christ rather than the ways of the world.

This revelation leads us to wonder if God gives each of us what we need in the way of extraordinary experiences in order for us to finally be able to see the truth. Of course, he also gives us "free will" to choose not to see, and we must each decide which side of the line we will stand upon. Whatever our experiences may be, God gives each of us the revelations we need to have in order to understand that he is sovereign. Whether we pay attention to these clues or not is up to each of us.

MILITARY SERVICE, A NOBLE CALLING

Our active and reserve military personnel are the men and women who guard the portals of freedom, and without them we would be very vulnerable to forces which would do us harm. There was a time not too long ago when our military personnel were not respected the way they are now. That time was during the height of the opposition to the Vietnam War. It was a time when our U.S. military personnel in uniform were disrespected and cursed in public. It was a disgraceful thing and we must never let it happen again.

Even in recent times we have seen people show a lack of respect for some of our veterans and active duty personnel. There was an exchange of words that took place between Senator John Glenn and Senator Howard Metzenbaum on the Senate floor on January 26, 2004, that illustrates the point. The exchange has been reported as follows:

SENATOR METZENBAUM: How can you run for the Senate when you've never held a real job?

SENATOR GLENN (D-OHIO): I served 23 years in the United States Marine Corps. I served through two wars. I flew 149 missions. My plane was hit by anti-aircraft fire on 12 different occasions. I was in the space program. It wasn't my checkbook, Howard; it was my life on the line. It was not a nine-to-five job, where I took time off to take the daily cash receipts to the bank.

I ask you to go with me, as I went the other day, to a veteran's hospital and look those men, with their mangled bodies, in the eye, and tell them they didn't hold a job!

You go with me to the Space Program at NASA and go, as I have gone, to the widows and orphans of Ed White, Gus Grissom and Roger Chaffee, and you look those kids in the eye and tell them that their dads didn't hold a job.

You go with me on Memorial Day and you stand in Arlington National Cemetery, where I have more friends buried than I'd like to remember, and you watch those waving flags. You stand there, and you think about this nation, and you tell me that those people didn't have a job?

As Colonel Glenn stated so eloquently, our soldiers and sailors and airmen do have jobs, and their jobs are probably the most important jobs that this nation has to offer. Colonel Glenn may have been reminded during this exchange with Metzenbaum of the disgraceful way he and other Vietnam Veterans were treated during the war. Hopefully that kind of behavior is completely behind us now, but we should be on guard against it ever raising its ugly head again.

Today I see young men and women in uniform being applauded in airports as they disembark from airplanes and walk through terminals, and I pray that it will always be so. Unfortunately, as the war in Iraq becomes more and more unpopular, and the anti-war movement grows; there is a danger that some protesters will again begin to blame our warriors for the war. We must never allow that to happen again. Sometimes when I say that we must never let it happen again, people will ask me "how can we stop it should this practice begin to reemerge?" The answer is that we must speak up the way Senator Glenn spoke up. Our elected officials, our business leaders, and our leaders in education must all speak up and say we "will not tolerate it." And we must say it over and over again until we have shamed those who would voice such disrespect against our men and women in uniform.

I am not saying that protest should not be tolerated. On the contrary I believe that lawful protest is an essential element of a free society. In fact the right of protest is a very important part of what our soldiers have always been willing to fight and die for. It is part of what keeps us free, but when the protesters turn on the very ones who are willing to fight to preserve that freedom then they have crossed the line.

Military service has always been a noble calling for our young people in America. Citizen soldiers have answered the call to arms consistently, and have performed admirably during national emergencies, returning to their civilian lives when the emergency is over. As was noted earlier the "war on terrorism" seems to offer endless opportunities for such service. We must continue to recognize the value of this service as a people and a grateful nation if we are to defeat those sinister forces that now seem dedicated to destroying our way of life.

LESSONS IN FAITH LEARNED
ON THE BATTLEFIELD

In future chapters I will share how the experience of war shaped my belief in God and demonstrated for me certain principles of faith that have continued to prove reliable through the years. Together, we will explore how each of these principles of faith applies to our lives, develop our character, and establish our individual moral fabric. We will also see how God speaks to us during times of conflict, danger, and distress. We will see how our moral fabric is tested during these times, and how God will reveal himself to us and disclose his plans for us. We will explore matters of conscience, and particularly those matters of conscious that might present moral dilemmas in times of war and strife.

THREE

The Sixth Commandment and a Just War

Praise be the Lord my Rock, who trains my hands for war, my fingers for battle,...
—Psalm 144:1

The night was very dark. In an undeveloped country such as Vietnam, nights are much darker than they are in developed countries such as the United States, and this was a very dark night with heavy clouds obscuring the moon and the stars. We had been sitting out there in the dark for several hours, and my eyes had adjusted to the lack of light so that I had achieved maximum night vision. I was sitting on the edge of a rice paddy, facing east with the Vam Co Dong River at my back.

The rice paddy stretched out some distance, probably 400 to 500 meters, to my front. To my left sat Sergeant Crutchfield, his weapon resting across his knees. He was staring intently towards the line of brush that was about twenty meters to our left. The brush line concealed a small stream that ran down the entire left side of the rice paddy and flowed into the river. The brush also concealed fourteen heavily armed South Vietnamese soldiers, who were lined up along the bank of the stream. That stream was where we expected that the enemy, the Viet Cong, would come as they made their way either toward or away from the river. Our intelligence people had told us that they had been using it as cover as they moved to attack various South Vietnamese Government and American military targets.

In the dim light I could see to my right the vague form of Sergeant Nea, our Vietnamese interpreter, who was stretched out on the ground with his head propped up on his helmet. Behind him lay the Vietnamese second lieutenant, my counterpart and commander of this operation. I thought I could hear the lieutenant softly snoring. Farther to my right, on a bare spot of ground sat three Vietnamese soldiers, our headquarters security element. Where these three soldiers sat there was very little vegetation between them and the river. Where Sergeant Crutchfield and I were sitting, there were low trees between the river and us. The time was about 2300 hours and the date was August 30, 1969.

As I surveyed the situation, I was reminded of the events that had occurred earlier in the day that had brought us to this place. A call over the radio came early in the morning from district headquarters, relaying orders for Sergeant Crutchfield, called Whitey because of his white hair, and me to report to U.S. Navy Headquarters that afternoon. We were told to come armed and equipped to conduct a night operation with a Vietnamese Regional Force platoon.

We had arrived at the naval dock at the appointed hour to find our commander, Major Jones, the Vietnamese second lieutenant, and Captain Poe, the Navy Commander, waiting for us in a small aluminum boat that was powered by an outboard engine and piloted by a Navy seaman. Whitey and I climbed aboard and we headed down river in a southerly direction. It was a sunny day with high cumulus clouds floating above, making the ride very pleasant. We passed numerous Vietnamese craft of various sizes plying up and down the river. The land along the river was primarily devoted to rice paddies, and peasants were out working in their fields.

After a ride of about thirty minutes, the Major asked the seaman to cut the engine and then stood up in the boat. He faced east and stretched out his arm, pointing toward a spot along the bank. Whitey spoke up sharply, "Sir, don't point. You will show all these gooks where we're going." The Major sat down and said, "There's a stream on the east side of the river. We believe the VC are using it to infiltrate the area, and I want you to set up an ambush there tonight to stop them." I had been on night ambushes before and most had been rather unsuccessful, but this one promised to be different. There seemed to be real intelligence behind the plan and the area looked like an ideal place for the VC to be moving back and forth across the border between Vietnam and Cambodia, which was only a few kilometers west of the river.

Back at Navy Headquarters we reviewed the plans for the operation with Major Jones, Captain Poe, Whitey, the Vietnamese lieutenant and me all giving our input. I was dismayed to discover that Major Jones did not know the most basic elements of conducting a night ambush, but decided not to make an issue of his ignorance and just conduct the operation in the proper manner once we got out into the field. Following this discussion, I was also a bit worried about my counterpart, the Vietnamese second lieutenant. He was very young and apparently inexperienced.

Prior to departing for the operation, we all met back at district headquarters to have dinner. Whitey, Nea, the Vietnamese lieutenant and I ate together in the large dining room that was situated in the middle of the complex of sand bag bunkers that comprised District Headquarters. After the meal, which was not bad by Army standards, I turned to Nea and asked him to speak to the Vietnamese lieutenant for me. "Tell him," I said, "that it is very important for our men to stay awake tonight on this ambush." Nea translated and received a rather hesitant response from the lieutenant. Addressing the lieutenant with the Vietnamese word for second lieutenant, Nea said, "Tieu uy says that the men must work during the day, so they sleep at night."

I knew that it was not unusual for the Vietnamese soldiers to sleep while on ambush, but I felt that this operation was special and suspected that our chances of encountering the enemy were greater than usual. I did not want them to be surprised. "Tell Tieu uy that if the VC come they will kill us if we are asleep." After a brief exchange of words with the lieutenant, Nea responded, "He says we must all die sometime. Who can tell when it may come?"

"It is more likely to come if we are all asleep," I responded, but did not pursue the matter any more, thinking that I would just do my best to keep them awake when we got out on the ambush. This philosophy of fatalism was, and I expect still is, widespread in Asia, and I had learned that I would not change centuries of ingrained philosophy with one conversation. Nevertheless, I was determined to do the best I could to keep it from getting us all killed.

When it got dark we went down to the Navy dock to meet with Tieu uy's platoon. After we had all climbed aboard, I did a count of the number of Vietnamese soldiers. According to the Major we were supposed to have at least twenty men and there were only sixteen, so I called HQ on the radio and told him we were short. He said that he would have his Counterpart, the District Chief, send over some more. After about fifteen minutes the lieutenant came to me and said that he now had the required number. I did another count with all the men filing past as I counted them. As I counted, I looked over my shoulder to see that some of the men were doubling back and jumping into line to be counted again. After sorting it all out, I determined we had picked up two more, giving us a total of eighteen men. When I called the major to give him the count, his response was, "Well, it looks like that is all you are going to get. If you are afraid, you don't have to go." The remark made my blood boil. "We'll go anyway," I answered.

As we began moving down the river in the PT boat, I noticed that heavy clouds had covered the sky, and as we left the bright lights of the Navy dock, I began to realize how dark it was. I could barely make out the black outline of the riverbank as we motored down the middle of the river. Despite the darkness, the pilot of the boat managed to deftly pull into the bank of the river and deposit our small force at the appropriate spot without incident.

As I had expected, the Vietnamese lieutenant positioned the bulk of his men along the stream bank where they could effectively bring fire on any enemy personnel who might be coming from either upstream or downstream. As I have previously described, Whitey, Nea, the lieutenant, three soldiers, and I were positioned near the riverbank where we could observe both the stream and the river. It was a classic setup, and I felt good about it until I observed that everyone except Whitey and I were apparently going off to sleep. With midnight approaching, I knew from my previous talk with the lieutenant it would be hard to keep them awake.

I was about to lean over and nudge Nea when I noticed a light to our east on the horizon and heard rumbling sounds that seemed to be coming from several miles away. A soft rain had begun to fall, and the light appeared as a faint glow in the hazy atmosphere. I picked up the mike to the radio, which was sitting on the ground next to me, and called district headquarters to inquire as to what was going on. The radio operator responded that an American artillery base was under attack, and that we should be on the lookout for any enemy units that might be moving to join in the attack or for elements that might be returning our way.

I passed the news to Whitey and then awoke Nea by kicking the sole of his boot. He jumped up, startled from his napping. I told him to inform the lieutenant of what was happening. Upon hearing the news, the lieutenant quickly went to the streambed to caution his troops. I was happy that this little flurry of activity had at least gotten every one up and alert. I reported back to headquarters that we were all alert and watchful for any enemy movement. For a short while the excitement served to keep everyone awake, but soon after midnight they settled down again, and I began to worry that fatalism would take over, and my companions would once again drift off into dreamland.

At about 2400 hours, I heard a faint bumping sound that seemed to be coming from upriver. I turned to Whitey and whispered, "What is that?"

He answered, "I don't know."

We listened intently for about a minute to the sound, which was of wood rhythmically bumping against wood, and then we both softly spoke at the same time, "A boat!"

I leaned over and nudged Nea. "Tell Tieu uy there is a boat on the river."

Nea did so, and the lieutenant moved a little to where he could see around the trees and down the river. He immediately crawled back and spoke to Nea. "He says it is VC. What must he do?"

For just a second I pondered the absurdity of the question. Here we sat, twenty-one men, holding about 1000 pounds of weapons and ammunition and he asked, "What should he do?"

In a low but firm voice I said, "Shoot 'em."

Translation was not necessary and the lieutenant yelled fire in Vietnamese. We all began firing on the boat that by this time was right in front of us. After a few minutes of deafening roar from our weapons, the lieutenant ordered his men to stop firing, and I saw only the empty boat turning in a circle in the water. Suddenly, the silence was broken by the sound of firing coming from the other side of the river, and bullets began to tear through the trees in front of us. By now, Tieu uy had brought the rest of his patrol to our position on the riverbank, and they returned fire on the enemy. I reported our situation to headquarters over the radio. I reasoned that the men we had shot were the lead element of a larger force that was being ferried across the river to join in the fight that was raging to our east. That force was now training their fire on our position, having determined that we must have stopped their men in the first boat.

After about a twenty-minute exchange of firing across the river, Captain Poe appeared with two PT boats and opened up on the enemy with 50-caliber machine guns. This ended the fight, and the enemy withdrew to the west, back towards Cambodia. Once the fight was over, our men retrieved three enemy bodies from the river, along with several weapons, ammunition, and documents. We knew there had been more but could not find them in the dark. We thought some had been shot as they tried to escape through the trees on the bank, but a search of the area turned up nothing. I would find out three days later that an American unit searching the area, found two freshly dug graves where farmers had apparently buried two more of the slain enemy. We all climbed aboard the boats and returned to naval headquarters.

YOU SHALL NOT MURDER

Back at the Navy yard, some of our soldiers laid out the three dead VC face up on the dock. I looked down at the one closest to where I was standing, and as if on cue, the full moon popped out from behind the clouds bathing the scene in a cool blue light. I looked at the face of this rather handsome young man whom I had helped to kill just a couple of hours before. Many thoughts began to rush through my mind. I thought about the uncertainty of life, about how if things had been just a little different I could be the one lying lifeless there on the dock. It occurred to me that this slain enemy soldier would never again experience the sunny days and warm nights of this tropical land, never again see his loved ones, and never know his unborn children.

I thought about his soul. Had it left his body to be with God, or was it forever trapped somewhere dark and sad? Paradoxically, at that moment I felt sorry for the loss of his life, but I did not really regret killing him. It was my job, just as it had been his job, and I knew that had the situation been reversed, he would have done the same to me. I looked up at the bright moon. I wondered if he was with God, could he see me standing there? Could God see me standing there, unrepentant and unforgiven?

I wasn't fully aware of it at the time, but I was having my second wake-up call. I was again forced to consider my own mortality while looking at the face of my fallen foe. A voice deep in my conscience was saying, "That could be you. Are you really ready to meet your maker? Are your hands clean? Have you killed your fellow man in violation of God's commandment?"

The sixth of the Ten Commandments, as handed down by God to Moses, is an admonition against taking the life of a fellow human being (Duet. 5:17). The original King James Version of the Bible says, "Thou shalt not kill." The Revised Standard Version says, "You shall not kill," while the more modern translations of the New Revised Standard Version and the New International Version both provide us with, "You shall not murder." On the surface they all seem to say the same thing but there is a subtle difference that has caused disagreement among theologians. The modern substitution of murder for kill has been used to justify acceptable, authorized killing as opposed to unacceptable, criminal murder. Modern theologians say that the best translation of the earliest texts is murder not kill.

The Old Testament provides numerous examples of the difference. Cain in the book of Genesis offers us the first example of a sinful killing, when he dispatches his brother Abel. This is obviously a case of murder with the motive of jealously, and God marks Cain for life as punishment. David on the other hand kills Goliath with the apparent approval and help of God. Later however David unrighteously causes the death of Uriah the Hittite in order to steal Uriah's wife Bathsheba. God condemns David for this murder and punishes him by taking the life of his infant son. Also, in the Old Testament, God himself orders the deaths of thousands of people and whole nations as the Israelites battle their way across the Promised Land.

In modern times we would say that a police officer killed an armed robber in the line of duty, but we would say that an armed robber murdered the shopkeeper while robbing his store. When it comes to war, we presume that the taking of life in battle is authorized killing and not murder, but it is not quite that simple from a purely moral point of view. There are those Christians who would say that war itself is immoral, and killing in war is never justified. While participating in a Christian mission trip to Vietnam in 2006, I met two men who explained that they had come to Vietnam in the early sixties as Mennonite missionaries because their religion does not permit killing, even in wartime. They readily admitted, however, that they appreciate being protected by those who choose to serve and fight when needed.

There is also a not so subtle difference between killing combatants in battle and the wanton killing of civilians, captives, and other non combatants, which are acts of homicide that are officially referred to as atrocities. Atrocities will be discussed in chapter 4, which deals with the forces of evil that prevail in war time, but it should be said now that this type of killing cannot be tolerated and is more akin to murder, even in a wartime setting.

THE NEW TESTAMENT

As Christians we must go beyond the Old Testament and ask what did Jesus say? In Matthew 5:21 he says, "You have heard that it was said to the people long ago, 'Do not murder, and anyone who murders will be subject to judgment.' But I tell you that anyone who is angry with his brother will be subject to judgment." Once again the operative word, as translated by the NIV, is murder. But Jesus goes a step further and says one who is angry at his fellow man is also guilty of a sin. Anger is a powerful tool of the Devil, and we must try to avoid this unproductive emotion. A soldier who allows anger to take him over is in danger of moving away from doing his duty and moving toward committing atrocities (murder). In Matthew 5:39 Jesus goes a step further by saying "... if someone strikes you on the right cheek, turn to him the other also." And then in Matthew 5:44 he says, "But I tell you: Love your enemies and pray for those who persecute you." As Christians, how do we reconcile this nonviolent and peaceful philosophy of our Lord and Savior against the reality of the need to defend ourselves in a potentially violent and dangerous world?

Although there are exceptions, such as my Mennonite friends, most people today agree that there are times when people may legally and morally kill fellow human beings in self-defense or during times of war. The events of 9/11, in fact, have hardened many peoples' views; as they realize that to some degree we all live in a world that can visit violence on us at any time, even on this side of the Atlantic. Nevertheless, a soldier who is faced with the reality, not just the philosophical nuances, of having to dispatch his fellow man, is likely to have some second thoughts, if not outright anguish, over the experience.

Chris Hedges has written a book entitled *Losing Moses on the Freeway*, which discusses all of the Ten Commandments from a modern point of view.[1] A veteran war correspondent and former theological student, he does an admirable job of exploring this subject in a chapter entitled "Murder." As part of his research, he interviewed Bishop George Packard, an Episcopal priest who has served as the Episcopal Church's bishop to the armed forces. As a young man, Bishop Packard was a first lieutenant in the U.S. Army. As a platoon leader in Vietnam, he led scores of ambush patrols that he says killed a very large number of the enemy. After he returned to the United States, he suffered a personal moral crisis that left him guilt ridden over the destruction of life that he had caused in Vietnam. This moral crisis eventually led him to become a student at Virginia Theological Seminary and then later led him back to the U.S. Army as a chaplain.

His experience in the ministry has obviously lessened his distress, but Bishop Packard admitted in the interview that he still had moments of anguish over what he had done in Vietnam. Under any standard of acceptable, even honorable, conduct during wartime, the bishop has done nothing wrong. In fact, his is the kind of service that we honor, having earned him the Silver Star and two Bronze

Stars for valor. Yet despite his belief that he has been forgiven and cleansed through the blood of Jesus Christ, he still has personally felt called to seek atonement through his work and his service to others as a chaplain and priest. The Bishop's experience attests to the fact that many of us who kill in combat are likely to experience some sort of anguish no matter how honorably we may have taken up the task.

As I have mentioned before, I had some unsettled feeling that night on the dock at Go Da Ha, and I have had many more since. At times even today I will occasionally find myself questioning my right to call myself a Christian. I will be sitting in Sunday school class or in a church meeting wondering if I am the only one in the room who has killed someone. Sometimes I ask myself, "Do I really belong here?" How then do we resolve this seeming disconnect between our Christian teachings of brotherhood and good will toward men and our need, or more precisely our duty, as soldiers to kill other human beings? The answer is that we all have to find sound moral ground upon which we can comfortably stand.

MORAL GROUND

After much reflection and study I have reached the conclusion that in my case I did kill but I did not murder. I went to war as a soldier serving in the armed forces of my country. Those who are supposed to make the monumental decisions about the justification for war, had trained me, and sent me into a hostile environment of kill and be killed. Notice that I did not say kill or be killed, because war is not necessarily a situation where you must kill in order to avoid being killed. War is not a shoot-out at the OK Corral, or a quick draw contest. Usually, it is not even a case of personal self-defense. Real war is more often like the ambushes Bishop Packard (then Lieutenant Packard) conducted, and like the ambush I described in the beginning of this chapter. It is more often a situation where we catch the enemy in an unfavorable position and we kill him. At a later date he may catch us in an unfavorable situation and kill us. Additionally, death and destruction takes place when bombs, artillery, or mortar rounds come falling from the sky, landing on us or the enemy, killing or injuring people indiscriminately. Particularly in today's "limited wars," battle is seldom a case of self-defense where soldiers are shooting it out with each other and they must kill or be killed. Winston Churchill said, "War, which used to be cruel and magnificent has now become cruel and squalid."

There is considerable danger in having a soldier become too conflicted over this moral dilemma in a combat zone. A soldier cannot afford to hesitate. He must act quickly and confidently in a combat situation. At the critical moment in our ambush described earlier, the Vietnamese lieutenant asked me what should he do, and I immediately responded, "shoot 'em." Let's suppose for a minute that I had said something different. Suppose, for instance, I had whispered, "be quiet and let them pass." What might have happened? The quick answer, of course, is that I would have been forsaking my duty as a soldier and not performing the job I had been sent there to perform, but let's look at the other possibilities.

If we had not fired when we did, it is possible that the enemy in the boat might have seen us on the bank as they passed by and opened fire, killing and wounding many of our people. In that case, we would have lost the element of surprise and would not have been able to complete the mission without losses on our own side.

Another possibility is that we may have caused a much larger loss of life among other friendly personnel had we stayed quiet. After we shot the five enemy soldiers in the boat, we began to receive a large amount of small arms fire from the other side of the river, indicating that there was a larger force there that most likely also intended to cross over to our side. Had we stayed quiet, they would surely have crossed over, and it is my belief that they would have joined the battle that was raging to our east at the American artillery base. The addition of their numbers may have turned the tide of battle, allowing the enemy to overrun this fire base, resulting in the deaths of many Americans. Additionally, if the entire enemy force had been allowed to cross the river, and then had discovered us on the bank, we would have been forced into a firefight with a larger unit, possibly sustaining a significant number of casualties. Depending upon the size of this enemy force, they may have been able to wipe us out and then still proceed on to attack and overrun the American firebase.

As it turned out, we were able to accomplish the mission and prevent losses in our own ranks, through quick and unhesitant action. A soldier cannot afford to have doubts or be hesitant in a combat zone. Therefore, he must be certain that he knows that he is on firm moral ground, and that he is doing the right thing.

Each soldier must deal with the necessity to kill in wartime in his own way. In my case, I resolved that I would fight as well as I could, but that I would not unnecessarily cause the loss of life if I could avoid it, and that I would never purposely attack innocent civilians or non combatants, and that I would always treat captives the way I would want to be treated if the situation were reversed. I determined that I would aggressively pursue and eliminate the enemy as a fighting force whenever I could, but I resolved not to commit murder (atrocities). I further decided that it was not my job to determine whether or not my country had involved me in a just war. That determination was not my assignment. My leaders, my President and my Congress, had that responsibility under our constitution, and they had already exercised that power. I had to trust that they knew what they were doing.

Many people have declared themselves to be conscientious objectors and still have performed valuable service for their country. Some have served as medics and many of these have performed heroics on the battlefield saving the lives and limbs of their wounded companions. Our Mennonite friends from the mission trip to Vietnam both served as missionaries there as alternative service in the 1960s. We should give due respect to all of those who by conscience decide to refrain from any service that may involve violence and who choose to serve in other ways. That being said, a nation that decides to be totally passive and nonviolent, is a nation that has decided by default to live in subjugation to others.

In summary, I believe that a soldier who does his duty and attacks the enemy in combat is not committing murder. That position may be too simple for some, but we still actually live in a fairly simple world when we consider moral issues. There is a quote that has been variously attributed to both George Orwell and Winston Churchill. It says, "We sleep soundly in our beds only because rough men stand ready in the night to visit violence on those who would do us harm." Unfortunately, this is still an imperfect world, where swords have not yet been beaten into plowshares, and someone must stand ready to defend our way of life and our very lives. Those defenders are the men, and now women, who serve in our military, and their service is both honorable and necessary and may from time to time involve the visiting of violence on those who would threaten us. In the final analysis it is a job that must be done, and it would be dangerous for us to begin to think that as a nation we can exist without their protection in a world where our enemies have shown us that they would kill us all in our sleep if they ever have the opportunity.

SIN AND ATONEMENT

What are those soldiers to do who still feel guilt or anguish over what they may have done, or not done, in combat? The simple answer is that they must do what we all must do if we think we have done something wrong. The Bible says, "For all have sinned and fall short of the glory of God...." (Romans 3:23). If we have all sinned, and we have, then we must all confess our sins and ask God for forgiveness. It does not matter how grave the sin. Forgiveness is available for all. The Apostle Paul tells us in 2 Corinthians 5:19 that, "God was reconciling the world to himself in Christ, not counting men's sins against them. And he has committed to us the message of reconciliation."

Consequently if we confess our sins and ask forgiveness, we are accepted as we are by grace, not earned but freely given. Paul explains further, "Therefore, since we have been justified through faith, we have peace with God through our Lord Jesus Christ, through whom we have gained access by faith into this grace in which we now stand" (Romans 5:1). If a person confesses his guilt and accepts God's forgiveness through the blood of Christ and still has feelings of conscience, it may be that this person needs to do some sort of atonement. This is not done for salvation, "For it is by grace you have been saved, through faith—and this not from yourselves, it is the gift of God—not by works" (Ephesians 2:8).

Bishop Parker had to do this even though he surely knew that he was saved. He chose to do atonement by devoting his life to helping other soldiers with their spiritual journeys and by bringing other people to Christ. John Newman, the author of the hymn "Amazing Grace" gave up a life of sin in the slave trade, became a priest and devoted the rest of his life to Christ. In the movie "Amazing Grace" Newman appears briefly at the end where he says, "I have been a great sinner but Jesus is a great Savior."

Sometimes God puts this on our hearts, and we know in our hearts that there is something we can and must do for atonement even though we are saved. Henry Blackaby says in *Experiencing God Day-by-Day*, "We were not saved from our sin simply so that we would qualify for heaven. God delivered us so we could have a relationship with Him through which He could carry out His mission to redeem a lost world."[2]

Atonement is part of the reason I am writing this book, part of the reason I went back to Vietnam on a mission trip, and part of the reason I will look for other ways to do God's will. Although I do not feel that I broke the sixth commandment by fighting the war, I do recognize that there has been plenty of sin in my life before, during and after Vietnam. I have repented, asked for forgiveness, and received the salvation of Christ, but there are still things that God has put on my heart to do in order to advance his Kingdom. I know that my life will be incomplete if I do not do what I can, insignificant as it is, so that God can complete his work in me.

I know that we have not completely solved the issues surrounding the Sixth Commandment and war, but in the end, it is the individual who must decide where he stands, and what he needs to do in order to personally face his God. For some no threat is so great and no cause is so worthy as to justify the taking of the life of another. For others, their freedom, the safety of their families, and their way of life are all too precious to let them stand by and not take up arms when these things are threatened. I firmly believe that a people who beat their swords into plowshares in this world that we now live in, will eventually labor for tyrants. No matter where we are on this subject, it is always more complicated if we find that the war we are called to fight is not a worthy cause. Therefore, the remaining question is, What is a just war, a war worthy of expending the blood and treasure of our nation?

A JUST WAR

Many years after the Vietnam War, I took up this question regarding the justification of war and considered it from three perspectives. First I needed to resolve in my own mind whether that Asian conflict that we call the Vietnam War, now called the American War by the Vietnamese, was justified. Secondly, I hoped that through study and reflection, I could discover a list of clear just war precepts that might guide us as Christians in the future when our country is again faced with the possibility of going to war. Thirdly, I hoped to apply those precepts to the current wars being waged in Afghanistan and Iraq in order to test their validity.

Our notions about what constitutes a just war are rooted in the writings of St. Augustine, a Christian Church leader and theologian who lived in the fourth century A.D. Augustine said that war is bad, a sin and the result of sin, but may have to be used occasionally as a remedy for sin. He wrote, "We go to war that we may have peace."

From him we get the notion that, "war is always wrong but some-times necessary." From him we also get our idea that war may be used to protect the innocent from aggression. These criteria sound noble, but do they suffice today as a guide to discerning justifiable wars from the other kind?

In the thirteenth century St. Thomas Aquinas affirmed the writ-ings of Augustine, but unfortunately, the philosophies of both men have been used over the years by European kings to declare war for their own selfish ends. The "king's peace" was extended by many monarchs to subjects and potential subjects as a means to avoid war, but what these despots were really saying was, "If you accept my rule over you and your lands, you will enjoy my peace. However, if you do not accept my rule, you will have war, and of course I prefer peace." The "Peace of Rome" lasted for almost a thousand years, but was for the most part preserved by the sword as it subjected thou-sands of people to servitude.

We must always be skeptical of national leaders who talk about wanting peace at the same time that they threaten war. As an example, Edward Longshanks, King of England in the thirteenth century, extended this offer of "peace or else" to Scotland. The Scottish people under the leadership of men like William Wallace rejected his offer and united under their own King, The Bruce, suc-cessfully defending their country against English rule. Today, world leaders still pontificate about peace while they pursue their own per-sonal or national policies that often ultimately lead to war, making it even more important for us to have a clear set of rules that we can all refer to when the parade drums begin to play.

JUST WAR PRINCIPLES

During modern times, the defining document that seeks to describe what constitutes a just war is "The Challenge of Peace: God's Promise and Our Response," a paper written and published by the U.S. Catholic Bishops in 1983.[3] Composed during the height of the Arms Race between the United States and the USSR, this document's main focus is the devastation that would be caused in the event of nuclear war. It also takes up the need for protecting innocents during the conduct of war, but we are most interested in a section entitled *Jus ad Bellum*, which explores, "Why and when recourse to war is permissible." The findings of this document are summarized below. Sub-quotation marks refer to quotes from the Second Vatican Council.

1. *Just cause:* War is permissible only to confront "a real and certain danger," i.e. to protect innocent life, to preserve conditions necessary for decent human existence, and to basic human rights.

This statement seems to justify war as a defensive action, that is, we may defend ourselves when attacked, the widely accepted concept that people, and nations of people, are entitled to self-defense. It might also be used to permit attacking a foe who is poised to do us harm, and this is where we start to get onto slippery ground. When we justify attacking a potential foe that is threatening us or may threaten us in the future, we get into gray areas of defining the reality and immediacy of the threat. The Vietnam War and the second war against Iraq are both examples of how this defense against a presumed threat has been used to validate wars. Our response to the attack by Japan on Pearl Harbor seems to be a clear example of a just declaration of war in response to unprovoked attack. On the other hand, the presumed existence of "weapons of mass destruction" was used in a not so clear justification for war in Iraq. Both situations were cast as justification for war as a means of self-defense, but they are certainly not equal in either gravity or consequence.

The phrase, "to protect innocent life," could be used to justify going to war to oppose any government or any enemy force that has attacked a weaker nation, particularly if that weaker nation is a friend. The Iraqi attack on Kuwait comes to mind, as well as the defense of Bosnia and our foray into Somalia. This high-minded rationale along with the charge to preserve "decent human conditions," raises the question of whether we should attack every despot who has suppressed and mistreated his people. Allies such as President Musharraf of Pakistan could be pulled into this wide net, as well as our formidable trading partner Red China. Fortunately, some of the other criteria put forth by the bishops limit just how far we may go with this self-defense argument.

> 2. *Competent Authority:* In the Catholic tradition the right to use force has always been joined to the common good; war must be declared by those with responsibility for public order, not by private groups or individuals.

This criterion can be interpreted in ways that are both limiting and expansive. It seems to limit the power to make war to legitimate governments, but the word government is not used. The word used is authority, which could be taken to include legitimate revolutionary organizations. Without this loophole, our own American Revolution would be unjustifiable.

The Bishops have included language in this section that acknowledges that some might assume a "Just Revolution" position. They say, "The mere possession of sufficient weaponry, for example, does not legitimize the initiation of war by 'insurgents' against an established government, any more than the government's systematic oppression of its people can be carried out under the doctrine of 'national security.'" Nevertheless the question of justifiable revolution is still open to interpretation.

In our country, the debate over the legitimate undertaking of war by our government centers around the need for a formal Congressional declaration of war before our military forces can be thrown against another country or government. The Constitution clearly calls for this, but it has been ignored in all of our recent wars, including the Korean War, The Vietnam War, the Afghanistan War, and both Iraq Wars.

U.S. Presidents have proceeded to war in each of these conflicts with only loosely worded congressional resolutions, not official declarations. This may seem to be only a matter of semantics but it is not. Our forefathers required a formal declaration of war for a reason. They wanted the President and the Congress to heavily weigh the issues of taking belligerent action towards another state. They wanted the people's interest to be duly considered, they wanted full debate, and they wanted the end result to be a solemn document declaring the full intention of the Nation, not just a vague resolution authorizing the President to do what he deems necessary.

3. *Comparative Justice:* Questions concerning the means of waging war today, particularly in view of the destructive potential of weapons, have tended to override questions concerning the comparative justice of the positions of respective adversaries or enemies. [This section of the document goes on to explain,] The question in its most basic form is this: do the rights and values involved justify killing? For whatever the means used, war, by definition, involves violence, destruction, suffering, and death.

Another way to frame the issue is to ask the question, which side has the "righteous cause?" The Vietnamese people, for instance have a strong sense of this concept of the "righteous cause," which had existed in their culture for hundreds of years before our involvement there. For most of their history the Vietnamese leaders who were viewed as possessing the "righteous cause" were the ones who opposed foreign influence and domination. This concept of "righteous cause" may be seen throughout their history as they opposed outsider attempts at domination, resulting in wars of resistance against China, Cambodia, Japan, and France. As an advisor with the South Vietnamese, I observed how this philosophy worked against us and our allies in the South Vietnamese Army.

4. *Probability of Success.* This is a difficult criterion to apply, but its purpose is to prevent irrational resort to force or hopeless resistance when the outcome of either will clearly be disproportionate or futile.

Presumably, this means a cause should not be taken up if the outcome is in considerable doubt.

5. *Proportionality:* In terms of the jus ad bellum criteria, proportionality means that the damage to be inflicted and the costs incurred by war must be proportionate to the good expected by taking up arms."

In an attempt to explain this principal by example, the Bishops state, "During the Vietnam war our bishops' conference ultimately concluded that the conflict had reached such a level of devastation to the adversary and damage to our own society that continuing it could not be justified." To further explain, they state, "The use of arms must not produce evils and disorders graver than the evil to be eliminated." Many people in this country today are arguing that this circumstance has been reached at this time in the prosecution of the second war in Iraq.

There are other church bodies that have attempted to define their positions on war. The United Methodist Church has provided a very succinct statement on the subject in *The Book of Discipline of the United Methodist Church* published in the year 2004. In a section called *War and Peace*, the Church summarizes its position as, "We believe that war is incompatible with the teachings and example of Christ. We reject war as an instrument of national foreign policy, to be employed only as a last resort in the prevention of such evils as genocide, brutal suppression of human rights, and unprovoked international aggression. We insist that the first moral duty of all nations is to resolve by peaceful means every dispute that arises between or among them; that human values must outweigh military claims as governments determine their priorities; and that the production, possession, or use of nuclear weapons be condemned. Consequently, we endorse general and complete disarmament under strict and effective international control." This statement certainly summarizes the nonviolent philosophy of Christ as presented to us in the New Testament.

WAR IN OUR TIME

The Just War: An American Reflection on the Morality of War in our Time by Peter S. Temes is a book that does an admirable job of exploring this concept of what constitutes a "Just War."[4] The book is based on the author's study and experience gained while teaching his course on the moral principles of war at Harvard University. Through this book, Temes provides a great deal of history about just war philosophy from ancient times to the present, and analyzes the religious just war positions of Judaism, Christianity, and Islam, the three great religions that trace their roots back to Abraham. He concludes his work by summarizing the principles of just war thinking that he views as having relevance for the twenty-first century.

First, he says that, "We must reaffirm the principle of noncombatant immunity."[5] This is a principle that seems more relevant to the conduct of war rather than to the decision to make war, but still it is important to keep in mind that wars by their nature often do more harm to innocents than to the combatants involved.

Secondly, he states that, "We must reaffirm the question of the legitimate authority."[6] He notes that "legitimacy is a complicated idea when applied to the notion of authority in time of war."[7] He gives Hitler and Saddam Hussein as examples of officially recognized national leaders who exercised their authority to wage war in a criminal fashion.

Thirdly, he considers the principal of "last resort" and concludes that, "The Catholic Just War principle of last resort is pointedly not among the criteria that I suggest we reaffirm."[8] He goes on to say that war must be avoided if possible, but points out that the things we do instead of war, "blockades, propaganda campaigns, and restrictions on trade—often create terrible harm for the weakest among an enemy nation's civilians while leaving the military and political leadership intact."[9]

Fourthly, he also rejects the Catholic Just War principle of "likelihood of success," noting that under this principle, our forefathers certainly would not have taken on Great Britain, the greatest military power of the time, when they declared our country free and sparked the American Revolutionary War. He notes, "that war is just only when the motive is so decent that to have fought the good fight and lost is preferable to have sat out and been spared."[10]

His fifth principal deals with the right of the individual to have safe passage, and the need to protect the environment, while the sixth "reaffirms the sanctity of all human life." Both are admirable rules for the civilized conduct of war but provide no meat in determining when war is justified.

In a section of the book entitled "A Just War Is a War about the Future Not about the Past," Temes contends that many of our conflicts today are the result of repressed hatred between peoples that may go back hundreds of years. He gives Kosovo as an example where a 500-year-old event, the conquest of Serbia by the Ottoman Empire, was the basis for a modern war that was unleashed by the demise of the Soviet Union. The fall of Saddam Hussein likewise has unleashed violent hatred between Sunnis and Shiites that had apparently been repressed by dictatorship for many years. The past should be forgotten he contends, and never be the focus for future conflict.

A JUST WAR POLICY TO LIVE BY

Now that we have explored this considerable block of information about just war philosophy, principles, and morality, it is important to condense it into a policy that we can live by as a nation and a people. Any attempt to establish hard and fast rules will of course be subject to valid criticism, but on the other hand, history has shown us that the absence of clarity and simplicity may lead us into murky territory where personal goals, political expediencies, and grandiose thinking can push us into destructive and costly military adventures.

Let us begin by making a clear distinction between rules for the civilized conduct of war and rules for determining when the undertaking of an act of war is justified. As for the conduct of war, the rule is simple. The lives and property of non-combatants (civilians, captives, and the wounded) should be preserved and protected to the greatest extent possible. This subject will be explored in the next chapter, which deals with atrocities.

My summary of just war policy follows:

1. *Legitimate authority.* In the United States of America there is only one legitimate method for undertaking war against another nation under the provisions of the Constitution. Congress must pass a formal declaration of war. As I have said before, this was mandated by the founding fathers for a reason. They wanted this most momentous undertaking to be fully debated and gravely considered by all the representatives of the people. We have strayed from this principal of late, to our detriment, and we need to return to it.

2. *Self-defense.* The best justification for war still rests on the principle of defense, or better-said, national self-defense. This justification would also apply when a friendly nation requires defending, particularly where a mutual defense pact exists with that friendly nation. This self-defense justification most clearly applies in the case of an

outright attack; the attacks on Pearl Harbor in 1941 and the New York Trade Center on 9/11/2001, being good examples. It would also apply where there is an imminent threat of attack, and this is where we could fall into murky waters. The threat should be truly imminent; the wolf should be at the door not roaming about in the forest or holed up in his den.

We are facing a dilemma now regarding Iran that may test this principle. If Iran does obtain nuclear weapons, we will be faced with the prospect of having a sworn enemy who has vowed to cause our destruction and the destruction of our ally Israel. If such a country should obtain nuclear weapons, the security of the entire world could be at stake.

3. *Last resort*. War should always be undertaken as a last resort after all other measures have been exhausted. As noted earlier, Peter Temes contends that the provisions that have been used against a state instead of war, such as embargos, will often harm the general population, particularly the poor, more than they will harm the leaders of a country. Unfortunately this is true, but total war is a more devastating malady for the people of the enemy country as well as our own people, than any political or trade sanctions that might be undertaken. I agree with the Methodist Church that war should not be used as "an instrument of national foreign policy."

4. *To protect innocent life*. Military action might be legitimately undertaken to protect and save innocent human life. Military action is currently being considered by the United Nations to prevent genocide in Darfur. It would be legitimate for the United States to join into this action if authorized by Congress, and this authorization might not be a formal declaration of war, but rather a resolution authorizing a specific action over a specific period of time. These military actions might be better characterized as "rescue missions" rather than war, and are usually best conducted under the umbrella of the United Nations.

There is a slippery slope here, however, that must be avoided.

The current war in Iraq has been justified recently as a war of liberation to remove a brutal dictator, Saddam Hussein. The question we must now ask is this: how far do we go with unseating dictators? I have previously spoken of the governments of Pakistan and China as having suppressed their people. Should we expend American blood and treasure in order to free these people of their oppressors? Obviously we cannot afford to depose every tinhorn dictator in the world who rules over a suppressed people. The latest estimate is that the war in Iraq will cost a total of about 3 trillion dollars before it is over. That is a pretty hefty price to pay if our only goal were to unseat a repressive dictator. Of course, the accompanying loss of life is another cost that must be weighed when we contemplate the efficacy of military action for this purpose.

A CHRISTIAN PERSPECTIVE

It is time now to answer the question, "What is a Christian to do?" Is it moral for a Christian, or any moral person for that matter, to enter into the military service of our country with the possibility that he or she, in doing so, might have to kill fellow human beings? Nowhere in the New Testament does Jesus ever say that we should take up arms against a foe. In fact, whenever he comes anywhere near the subject, his statements are more pacifist, saying that we must love our neighbor and turn the other cheek.

The problem is that his kingdom has not yet fully come, and we still live in a world where Jesus tells us that the Devil is the prince of the earth. We live in a world where our enemies fly airplanes into buildings just hoping to kill as many of us as possible. In such a world we must have protectors. Churchill said, "War is horrible but slavery is worse."

What should we do if we are asked to fight in a war that is unjust? No one should have to fight a war that he or she knows for certain is unjust. However, it would not do for each soldier to decide on the eve of battle that he will not fight because he has suddenly determined a war to be unjust in his own mind. When I went to Vietnam I knew that there were serious questions about the war, but I also knew that I was obligated to do my duty and serve my country, and that our leaders were responsible for determining the justification of the war. May the Lord help any President or other leader who ever puts our young men and women in harm's way without clear justification.

TODAY'S WARS

If we use the criteria that I have listed above to evaluate the wars we have fought in the twentieth and twenty-first centuries, what will we find? If we start with World War I, I believe that we can find ample justification for this war. It was a war fought to defend nations that were our allies, primarily Britain and France, against an aggressive foe, Germany. The Congress authorized the war with a proper declaration. The same can be said about World War II, with the added justification that we were actually attacked by one of our adversaries, Japan, at Pearl Harbor. We first declared war on Japan, and then Germany declared war on us.

When we consider the war in Korea, the picture is less clear. Although there was an authorizing resolution from the United Nations, there was no formal declaration of war by Congress. On the surface, the self-defense requirement seems to have been met since the North Koreans attacked our friends, the South Koreans, and our U.S. troops that were stationed there. But, for the meeting of this test to be valid, we would have to take up the question of whether it was valid and moral in the first place, for the world powers to have divided this ancient people into two separate states. That question is another whole subject that merits a considerable amount of study and analysis to answer. When a people decide to divide themselves for political purposes, that is one thing; but when other more powerful forces, in this case the communist and free world powers, do it, that is another thing entirely. Vietnam was another situation where an ancient, homogeneous people were divided along political lines by the same powers.

The Vietnam War, probably the most divisive war in our history since the Civil War, seems to fail most of the tests. There was no declaration of war from Congress. It was clearly not a case of self-defense. It was argued, and is still argued, that we needed to come to the aid of an ally, South Vietnam, which was under attack by North Vietnam and also under attack by an internal insurgency, the Viet Cong. As with Korea, the question that should be asked first is, was it right to separate an ancient people into two separate states? On reflection, I think that the answer is no. Given the same circumstances today, hopefully we would decide not to expend our country's blood and treasure on such an enterprise. Even Robert McNamara, President Johnson's secretary of defense, has now called the Vietnam War a mistake. This is a hard realization for me to accept, being a Vietnam veteran. People have said it is a shame to have died in such a war. I say it is also a shame to have killed in such a war.

The first Iraq war seems justified, except that there was no formal declaration of war by Congress. There was a clear case of aggression by a rogue state, Iraq, against our ally and trading partner, Kuwait. The war in Afghanistan also meets the test of self-defense, since men who were trained and directed by Al-Qaeda, which was headquartered in Afghanistan and assisted by the Afghan government, attacked us on September 11, 2001. A formal declaration of war by Congress would have made the enterprise totally legitimate in my view.

From the perspective of hindsight, the second war in Iraq seems to lack justification. There are now entire books devoted to both sides of the debate, but for our purposes in this discussion, we can say there was no imminent danger to our country, and the self-defense test was not met. The remaining question now is, how do we extract ourselves from this conflict without throwing the country of Iraq into complete discord and destruction? We are now experiencing the truism voiced by Niccolo Machiavelli when he said, "You may start a war when you like but you may not end it when you please." Now that we are there, we cannot just walk away without preparing our Iraqi allies to provide for their own security.

UNTIL THE KINGDOM COMES

As Christians we look forward to the coming of the Kingdom of God when there will be no suffering, no tears, no loss of loved ones, and no war, but that time is not here. In Mark 1:14, Jesus proclaims, "The time has come. The Kingdom of God is near. Repent and believe the good news!" Our time is not God's time. Jesus said that the time was near approximately 2000 years ago, and yet it has not yet arrived. Nicky Gumble, in his Alpha Course film series, says that the Kingdom of God actually started with Jesus' ministry on earth and is still growing. This is evident when we consider that since Jesus' death, the church has grown from a small number of believers, the twelve disciples and maybe 120 or so other believers, to where it is now estimated that there are approximately 1,900 million Christians in the world today. And although there have been some declines in the number of Christians in Europe, the number worldwide is still growing.

The Kingdom will be fully formed at the second coming when Jesus returns in power and glory (Mark 13:26). At that time we will exist in a perfect world where, "They will beat their swords into plowshares and their spears into pruning hooks. Nation will not take up sword against nation, nor will they train for war anymore" (Isaiah 2:4). In the meantime we must live in an imperfect world that is still birthing the Kingdom, and in that imperfect world we need protectors from those who would do us harm. Those protectors are our men and women in uniform. They must stand ready in the night to do their duty, to do violence if need be, against those who would take our freedom or our lives from us.

It is incumbent upon our leaders, our President and the Congress, to make wise decisions about when to sound the call to war and when to refrain from beating the war drums. History has shown us that our leaders do not always make the right decisions, and it is up to us, the people, to know the difference between just and unjust causes and to require our leaders to exercise good judgment as they perform their duty to protect our nation.

Until the Kingdom comes, we will continue to be subject to wars, and we will also be subject to other evils and to evil forces that make all of our lives more difficult. During times of war these evil forces become more pronounced, and Satan, the face of evil, becomes more visible. In the next chapter we will explore how we may see this evil more clearly and learn how we may defend against it.

FOUR

Spiritual Warfare

For our struggle is not against flesh and blood, but against the rulers, against the authorities, against the powers of this dark world and against the spiritual forces of evil in the heavenly realms.

—EPHESIANS 6:12

As the Senior Advisor of Mobile Advisory Team 66, I soon learned that one of my jobs was to investigate atrocities that occurred in my sector. There were two instances of this nature that required my attention during my tour. The first time was while we were still at Tra Vo. It was a day when I was sitting on my bunk inside the villa, cleaning my equipment. A Vietnamese soldier came running into the room and told me in a very excited voice that we needed a medical dust-off for a woman who was injured out on the highway. I went immediately to the radio and called in the dust-off. Then I grabbed a smoke grenade and asked the soldier to take me to the injured woman.

Highway number 22, the major road between Saigon and Tay Ninh City, ran right past the gate to our compound. The traffic was very heavy on this road and I assumed that a car or a truck had struck a pedestrian. When we reached the scene, I saw a small, older woman lying face up on the side of the road. The right side of her head was bloody and she appeared to be unconscious. "What happened?" I asked. The soldier who accompanied me spoke a fair amount of English and tried to explain what had happened.

"Helicopter came down from sky and hit woman," he explained. A very improbable image flashed through my mind of a helicopter, swooping down from the sky, smacking the old woman in the head, and returning to the sky. The woman appeared to be less than five feet tall, and it was hard for me to believe a helicopter had struck her. I questioned the soldier, who questioned other people who had witnessed the incident.

As more information came in, I began to believe this incredible statement, and the picture became clear. This spot on the highway was a bus stop where people congregated to catch the bus to Tay Ninh City. A U.S. chopper flew down the road, traveling south away from Tay Ninh toward Go Dau Ha. The pilot was flying low and buzzing the people along the road for sport. When he got close to the bus stop, he dropped down to just a few feet off the highway. Everyone except the woman heard him coming and dove to get out of the way. The woman was apparently hard of hearing and didn't jump. One of the skids of the chopper smacked her head, knocking her to the ground.

As I heard this story, I looked at the woman. She was not moving and appeared to be dead. She was about my mother's age, I thought. She was someone's mother, maybe a grandmother, and some asshole has probably killed her for no reason. As I thought about this, I was overcome with sadness. How could we ever hope to win the hearts and minds of these people if our men were doing things like this to civilians?

Soon the dust-off chopper was on the scene above, and I threw out the smoke, which was purple in color. I was so distracted by my thoughts that I threw the grenade up-wind. The smoke engulfed me like a fire. I breathed in the smoke and began coughing violently. The chopper came in, picked up the woman, and headed for the hospital. When I arrived back at the villa, the pilot came over the radio and said the medic on board wanted to know the cause of the injury.

"She was hit in the head by a chopper skid," I reported.

There was a long pause on the other end, and then the response was, "Really?"

"Roger," I said. "Some asshole dropped down out of the sky, smacked her in the side of the head, and took off."

Another long pause. "Roger."

I didn't know what happened to her, but I assumed that she died at the hospital. The next week, I was asked by headquarters to write a report, which I did. It was almost impossible to determine which of the many choppers in the air at the time did this hateful deed. I doubt that the pilot was ever found out, but I have always hoped that he was made to pay for this atrocity in some fashion.

Later, at Ben Cau I was asked to investigate the death of a Vietnamese boy who was reportedly killed by an American. The boy had lived in the neighboring village just south of Ben Cau, and Dai uy Tail, my Vietnamese counterpart, volunteered to take me there to meet the victim's father. We traveled on motorcycles, Dai uy and I each riding on the back of Hondas at a charge of twenty-five cents. We arrived there quickly and went directly to the home of the father. He was a farmer who lived on the edge of the village, in a small wooden house with a grass roof and a dirt floor. Like many other farmers, he lived in the village but would go out each day to work in the fields. He was a small, thin man, stooped at the shoulders from years of hard work in the rice paddies. His skin was dark and wrinkled from being in the sun all of his life. He was probably only in his late forties or early fifties, but he looked much older

Dai uy introduced me to the man, who bowed low and invited us into his home, which was minimally furnished with a small table, some low sleeping platforms, and an oil-cooking stove. The man gave me a low stool to sit on while he and Dai uy sat on their haunches in the Vietnamese style. I was amazed how this grieving father, having just lost his son, greeted me with respect and with no apparent anger or animosity. I had dreaded this meeting because I assumed that the father would take out his grief on me. I thought he would be resentful and angry toward me, but he was not. He seemed to be able to separate me from the American who had murdered his son.

As the father talked, Dai uy translated. He spoke very slowly, as though the words were painful, but he seemed determined to relate the events that surrounded the death of his son as witnesses had described them to him. As the man spoke and Dai uy translated, a picture of his son's death took shape in my mind.

The boy had risen before dawn, as was his custom, as was the custom for most of the village people. He had a brief breakfast with his mother and father and then prepared to go out for the day to watch over the small herd of cattle that belonged to the family. His mother handed him a handkerchief, containing two small rice cakes that would be his lunch. He put the corners of the handkerchief together and slid them under the rope belt that held up his baggy black pants, forming a little pouch by his side. He wore a faded brown T-shirt with three small holes in it that had been washed many times. As he left the cottage, he retrieved a slender bamboo rod from the side of the doorway that he used to prod the cattle in the direction he wanted them to go. He was fourteen-years old but small for his age.

As he stepped outside, he noticed that the sun was just barely rising above the treetops at the edge of the village. He went to the small pen next to the cottage and drove out the three animals, consisting of two large water buffalo and one milk cow. It was a routine they all knew well because it was what they did each day at this time of the year. At other times of the year, the rice paddies would be in cultivation, and buffalo would be working, but now the days consisted mostly of trying to find enough grass in the fields to fill their stomachs. These were mostly quiet, lazy days, and the boy and his charges all walked slowly down the trail past other houses to the edge of the village and out into the fields.

By the time the boy reached the field, the sun was bight and the day was already getting warm. He tried to find shade as the cattle moved about the field, snipping blades of grass. He stood first under one tree and then under another. Sometimes he squatted on his haunches under a tree. Other times he stood or squatted in the open in the hot sun. At times he had to go out and tap one of the animals with the slender bamboo rod and turn it back into the proper field.

On the way out to the field, the boy had noticed a large bevy of helicopters pass over. He knew from experience that this meant that the American soldiers would be looking for VC in the areas west of the village. He knew it was important to stay away from the soldiers, but it should be no trouble this day since they seemed to be landing far west of his location.

The father explained that war was a puzzle to them. They had seen the VC come and go, and sometimes he would hear them late at night as they passed close to his cottage. The war waged around his village at times, but for the most part, the villagers were not part of it. He had no idea what they fought about. The lives of his family members were what they had always been, hard days eking out a poor living from the ground. It did not matter to them who ruled in Saigon or who was running the country. Their lives were the same regardless, the same as it had always been for them and their ancestors for as long as anyone could remember.

About mid-morning, the boy's attention had lapsed. Looking up from a shady spot under a tree, he noticed that his animals had strayed across the field and needed to be turned back. He rose and started walking briskly across the field to retrieve them. When he was about halfway across, he noticed a small helicopter, circling high above the field. He stopped and looked up at it curiously. It began to descend rapidly. As he watched in amazement, it settled down on the ground in front of him. It was much smaller than the others that had flown over earlier, and it only held two men.

One of the men opened the door to the helicopter, stepped out, and rapidly walked over to him. The boy smiled at the man. He had only seen Americans up close a few times before, and they had never been a threat. The man was very tall and had very white skin like he had not been in the sun very much. He wore a clean, pressed, green uniform. He spoke to the boy, but the boy did not understand him.

The man seemed to be getting angry. He was asking for something, but the boy could not understand what. The boy said, "*Khong biet,*" meaning, "I do not understand." Finally the man produced a small card, pointing to it and the boy understood that the American wanted the boy to show him some identification, but he had none. He was merely a boy, the son of a poor farmer. He had no need for such things, so he only shrugged. Again he said, "*Khong biet.*"

The American became very angry and struck him, knocking him to the ground. Then the man reached over and grabbed the handkerchief from his belt, pulling it loose. The two rice cakes rolled out onto the ground. The man then walked back to the helicopter and flew away. The boy was frightened but relieved that the man had left. His first thought was to run home to his mother, but then he remembered the cattle. He would have to retrieve the cattle. By now they were well across the field, straying into someone else's territory where they would not be welcomed. He jumped to his feet and ran after them.

After only a few minutes, he had them rounded up and was driving them back across the field toward home. Then he saw the helicopter again. It was the same one with the same two men, and it descended quickly, falling toward him. He forgot about the cattle and began to run toward the village. As he ran, he heard a loud explosion behind him. Looking over his shoulder as he ran, he saw the same man, leaning out the window of the helicopter. The man threw a hand grenade at him. This grenade exploded closer than the first but still did not hit him.

The boy ran faster and weaved back and forth across the field as the man continued to throw more grenades at him, fortunately missing. There were other people at the edge of the field but they did not help, could not help. Finally, after several misses, one of the grenades fell close enough that several pieces of shrapnel hit the boy in the back and legs. The blast pushed him through the air and knocked him to the ground. He rolled over and looked back at his attacker. The chopper had landed, and the man was getting out with a rifle in his hands. Despite the pain and shock of his wounds, the boy rose to his feet and began to run again. The last thing he was heard to say before the man shot him was, "Mama."

I was so moved by the story that I couldn't speak. At first I was overwhelmed with anger, and then I was overwhelmed with great sadness. I knew that the war was full of such stories and that they were being played out all over the country. They had been replayed many times over the years. There were tragedies like this on both sides. There were also American boys being needlessly wasted, and most likely, the last thing they thought of was their mothers.

When he was finished with his story, the old man looked down at the dirt floor. I saw the top of his head. His hair was mostly gray and very thin. I felt extremely sorry for him. I thought he would probably like to cry, but his culture would not let him cry. I felt like crying myself, but my pride would not let me. I stood up. Dai uy also stood up and flashed me a nervous smile. I said, "Tell the father that I will write a report and try to make the man who did this answer for his action."

After Dai uy translated, I shook hands with the man and said, "*Toi xin loi*," which means "I am very sorry." I was glad that I could at least offer this brief apology in his tongue. He bowed low and smiled, seeming to appreciate the effort. Dai uy and I bowed and left.

After leaving the father's home we visited with two other farmers who had witnessed the killing. I wrote down their testimonies and thanked them for the information. Then Dai uy and I returned to our headquarters in the middle hamlet.

That night back in our bunker, I wrote out my report. I had made careful notes about the date and time of the incident, and I was careful to include these in the report. I also included the two eyewitness reports. I noted that the perpetrator of this crime was most likely an officer who was overseeing a large offensive operation on that day at that hour in that location. He was riding in the passenger seat of an LOH (light observation helicopter), which pegged him as a senior officer, probably a major or colonel. Anyone with access to the records should have been able to figure it out. I also made an inquiry of the American firebase in our area and discovered that there was a unit operating in the vicinity of the crime out of that base on that day. I hand-delivered my report to district headquarters the next day.

Several weeks passed and I heard nothing although I asked occasionally over the radio. One day after an operation, I was walking up the dusty road from the southern village, heading back to our bunker in the middle hamlet, when I passed the pay officer from headquarters. He was a finance captain, and each month he would come into our camp by helicopter with our pay already segregated into small envelopes. He would pass them out, take up money from any men who wanted to buy government bonds, and then take off to the next outpost. This day he was out in the hot sun, sweating profusely as he walked down the road. When we met in the middle of the road, I stopped and said, "Hello, Captain, what are you doing way out here?"

His answer was, "I'm going to the next village to pay off an old man whose boy was killed."

"How much is a boy worth these days?" I asked with much sarcasm in my voice.

He answered the question matter-of-factly as though it was not unusual. "Two hundred and fifty dollars." That was certainly a lot of money for a poor farmer, but I suspect some justice would have done more at that time to win over the people of Ben Cau.

I never found out if the officer who committed this atrocity was punished in any way or not. I hope that the payoff meant that he was, but most likely, the incident was swept under the carpet. I believe that the real cause of this tragedy was the relentless pursuit for body count that was still prevalent in 1969 even though the stated goal was pacification and Vietnamization. This incident clearly demonstrated to me why we were losing the larger struggle for the hearts and minds of the people, even though we were winning most of the battles.

Atrocities occur on both sides in every war. In this regard, Vietnam was probably no better or no worse than any of the other wars that American boys have fought. Although the two instances I have described both involved officers (a helicopter pilot, who was probably either a lieutenant or a warrant officer, and a commander, who may have been a major or a colonel), it is more often enlisted men in terms of numbers who are involved in these kinds of atrocities.

In every situation, it is always the officers who must control and direct the actions of their men. These things are less likely to happen if the men know that their immediate superiors will not tolerate them. The rule goes all the way up the chain of command. When there is a breakdown in leadership, then we have horrific incidents like the massacre at My Lai with Lt. William Calley, Jr., in Vietnam and national embarrassments like Abu Ghraib in Iraq.

As military conflicts drag on year after year as they did in Vietnam, the likelihood of atrocities grows. It is a difficult challenge for the officer leaders. We must encourage our men to do an unnatural, uncivilized thing—to kill. And yet try to keep them civilized at the same time. Our men must be both ruthless in their pursuit of the enemy and compassionate toward the innocent. It is a difficult, but essential, challenge. If soldiers are not controlled in this regard, some will invariably commit unspeakable acts. Some defenders of perpetrators will argue it is because of rage or frustration over the loss of comrades, but this is not a justification, and it must never be tolerated, particularly where noncombatants are concerned.

In addition to being a moral outrage that should not be tolerated, atrocities committed by our troops also have a deleterious effect on the outcome of our efforts in the occupied country. An army in the midst of an invasion, such as the invasion of Iraq, can suffer a few instances of improper behavior on the part of its combatants and not experience any long-term consequences (other than the obvious moral and, hopefully, legal consequences for those committing the crimes). However, when an army becomes an ally of the "host country," a euphemistic phrase for the occupied country, then the atrocities can and do have a long-lasting and detrimental effect on the war, or occupation effort.

Consider the old man in Ben Cau who lost his son. He was a gentle man and apparently took his $250 and went on with his life despite the loss of his son. Suppose, however, that he had been more resentful, as he had every right to be. Suppose he had bought an AK-47 with the money he received and had joined the resistance. Who would blame him? In fact, if you were his neighbor or his relative, would you not consider joining him?

We can easily take one damaged individual and multiply him into five or ten more recruits for the resistance. Sometimes well-meaning actions that are directed at the enemy go astray and cause the unintended deaths or wounding of innocents. These events also can serve to recruit or engender sympathy for the enemy. These mishaps are a normal consequence of war and, though they are often avoidable, they are more understandable.

These accidents will undoubtedly grow the insurgency, but when you add intentional acts of atrocities, the problem can grow from a small element of dissidents to a large and formidable force united by what is considered a righteous cause

THE CAUSE OF ATROCITIES

Whenever this subject comes up, some people will ask me what caused these atrocities to happen. The secular answer is easy. There is a criminal element in this society, and some of those criminal types naturally end up in the military. When given deadly weapons and left in relatively unsupervised situations, those individuals with criminal leanings will commit heinous acts.

A more fully honest answer is more complicated than this, and I believe involves the "spiritual forces of evil" that Paul talked about in the Ephesians 6:12 as quoted at the beginning of this chapter. More simply stated, it is the power of the Devil at work on this earth.

When I was a child growing up and attending church each Sunday, the Devil was hardly ever mentioned. The theology that seemed to prevail then was that God is love, supreme goodness; and nothing else of an evil nature could possibly share this space on earth or in the spiritual realm. In Vietnam I saw evil abound in incidents like the two described above. They occurred on both sides, and ranged from minor to horrible in severity. It was as though the evil had a life of its own, and I came to believe that it must be the work of the Devil. It actually helped me to believe in God, because I reasoned that if there is such a powerful element for evil in the world, there must also be an even more powerful force for good, or we should all be lost and without hope. Of course that more powerful force for good is God, as revealed to us by Jesus Christ, acting for good on the earth through the Holy Ghost.

The Devil, however, can only do his evil work on earth when he is allowed to enter the hearts of men. Let's take the American officer who killed the Vietnamese boy as an example. On the surface he was probably not the criminal type. He probably never robbed a gas station or convenience store. He had probably never criminally assaulted anyone, or committed fraud, or any of the other crimes we associate with the criminal mind. We know this because under our military system, a senior officer would have never achieved his rank with such a blemish on his record. He may have even been a respected family man, or possibly attended church back in the States.

Then why did this officer commit this atrocity? What went wrong? The answer is sin. Although we will never know the full circumstances, we can suspect that there was some sin in the man's life that he chose not to control. Perhaps he was angry because of something that had happened. Perhaps he had lost some of his men to the enemy, perhaps to a booby trap, or an ambush, or to a mortar attack. Perhaps he allowed the sins of anger and vengeance to enter his heart. There was a strong push for officers to increase their body count of the enemy, and he may have decided to take matters into his own hands. In this case his sins would be of pride and greed leading to the sin of murder. We do not know what his sin was, but we can be sure that sin entered into the man, and he allowed the Devil to take over.

OUR DEFENSE AGAINST THE DEVIL

The comedian Flip Wilson used to say, "The Devil made me do it." He used this humorous remark to excuse all sorts of little sins that he may have committed. Although he meant it to be humorous, Flip's remark has an important message for us. As implied by the statement, the Devil does cause us to commit sin, but he is not all-powerful. He merely presents us with the opportunity to sin. We do not have to defeat him because Jesus has already defeated him on the cross when he died for our sins. It is merely our job to resist the temptation to sin. The Apostle Paul gives us some weapons to aid us in this fight in Ephesians 6:13–17: "Therefore put on the full armor of God, so that when the day of evil comes, you may be able to stand your ground, and after you have done everything, to stand. Stand firm then, the belt of truth buckled around your waist, with the breastplate of righteousness in place, and with your feet fitted with the readiness that comes from the gospel of peace. In addition to all this, take up the shield of faith, with which you can extinguish all the flaming arrows of the evil one. Take the helmet of salvation and the sword of the Spirit which is the word of God."

Paul's message is that we must arm ourselves to foil the Devil and resist sin. The passage says we must arm ourselves "so that when the day of evil comes, you may be able to stand your ground." If this is so, what is the "day of evil?" You might say that it is every day. Wartime certainly produces more days of evil than we can imagine, but we know that we must be on guard every day, for everyday we are tempted, and as we have previously learned, we "are all sinners."

In the book of Job we are introduced to Satan, the Old Testament name for the Devil that means "accuser" in Hebrew. At first he seems like an almost harmless character that comes before the heavenly throne with the angles and enters into conversation with God. The Lord asks, "'…where have you come from?' Satan answered the Lord, 'From roaming through the earth and going back and forth in it.'"(Job: 1:7). Despite its seemingly harmless appearance, this scene gives us a useful picture of the Devil and his activity in the world. He is roaming about, patrolling in military terms, looking for opportunities to accuse us. He is looking for opportunities to trip us up. If we are prone to fits of anger he will throw anger-producing situations at us. If we are prone to lust he will confront us with lustful images. If we suffer from too much pride he will give us that temptation. Simply stated, it is our responsibility to resist. Despite what Flip says, the Devil cannot *make* us do anything.

FIVE

Courage

Be strong and courageous. Do not be terrified;
do not be discouraged, for the Lord your
God will be with you wherever you go.
—JOSHUA 1:9

I have known many courageous people in my lifetime. Some have been admirable people and some have not. Some have looked like heroes; tall, strong, and good looking. Others have not looked the part at all, but they have all possessed an indefinable ability to be courageous in times of danger, distress, and difficulty. There are three men in particular who come to mind, each quite different from the other, and each possessed a different brand of courage.

DANNY

When I finished my course of study at the Infantry Officers Basic School at Fort Benning, Georgia, I received orders to report to Fort Hood, Texas for my first duty assignment. Upon arriving at Fort Hood in June of 1968, I was assigned to a mechanized Infantry Company in the First Armored Division. At first I served as company executive officer under a young first lieutenant who had graduated from West Point. After only a couple of months in this position, I was made Company Commander when the first lieutenant left to go to Vietnam. Needless to say, I was very nervous about assuming this role as a brand new second lieutenant who had only been in the Army about five months.

As I began to serve in this command position, I soon learned that my greatest asset was a cadre of experienced NCOs (Non-Commissioned Officers) who were dedicated to their duty, seemed interested in helping me as much as possible, and did their best to keep me out of trouble. And there was plenty of trouble to go around. My inexperience would have been enough to cause me trouble, but in addition to this my company was full of enlisted men who had already been to Vietnam and were merely waiting for their enlistments to expire so that they could get out of the army and go home. They were not much interested in the daily training that the Army had prescribed for them to receive and that my NCOs and I were obligated to provide. In short, the morale of the men was terrible, and there was very little that any of us could do to motivate them.

One young man proved to be particularly troublesome. Danny had already been in trouble before I had arrived and had been demoted from Specialist 4 back to private. He was constantly doing things that landed him in front of my desk for disciplining. He disobeyed orders, failed to report for training, had been absent without leave on occasion, had been drunk and disorderly, and had received tickets from the MPs for improper driving on post. He also got into trouble in town with the civilian police. Once I was awakened in the middle of the night by a phone call from his mother asking that I go to the county jail where he was being held for drunk driving. I got dressed, called the local bail bondsman, and went to the jail to get him out.

Of all the problems I faced in this difficult command position, Danny seemed to be the most intractable. I gave him administrative punishment, which he readily accepted, in order to keep him out of formal court-marshal proceedings, but still he continued to get into more trouble.

Finally, one Monday morning he was missing from the morning formation. The next day he was still missing and the First Sergeant reported him as AWOL (absent without leave). After a week, there was still no word from Danny, and I was elated that I did not have to deal with him anymore. I thought that he had removed himself from my responsibility, and I was glad that he had done so.

After Danny had been missing for a little more a month, I received a call one morning from a sergeant at Fort Sill Oklahoma. He said that Danny had been picked up by the MPs there and had been in their stockade for about three weeks. He said that I needed to come and pick Danny up and bring him back to Texas. "Why don't you just keep him Sergeant," I said, "and deal with him there?" "No sir," he said, "He is your responsibility, and you need to come and get him." By now my first sergeant was standing in the doorway. He had been listening, and was shaking his head, indicating that I was not taking the proper position on the matter. "Ok," I said, "My First Sergeant will make the arrangements."

The next day Danny's platoon sergeant was in my office wearing dress khakis, carrying a 45-caliber pistol and preparing to go and get Danny. My First Sergeant had prepared orders to authorize the platoon sergeant to pick up Danny from Fort Sill and return him to our company. I signed the orders and sent him on his way with an authorization to pick up a car from the motor pool to make the trip.

Two days later the First Sergeant had Danny standing in front of my desk. From an appearance standpoint, he was a changed man. His uniform was neat and pressed and his hair was closely trimmed. He stood firmly at attention and saluted briskly. When I gave him the command "at ease," he moved into a sharp parade rest. I do not remember much of what was said, but his conversation was very respectful and he said that he was very sorry that he had caused so much trouble. I assumed that three weeks in the Ft. Sill stockade had taught him some manners. I dismissed him and told him that I would bring him back when I decided what to do with him. I knew that under military law he deserved a court-marshal and would likely pull some serious time in the stockade.

The next day, while I was pondering what to do with Danny, the company clerk dropped a pile of discharge papers on my desk that would release several of our men from the service because their enlistments were up. One of those discharge papers was Danny's. I looked it over carefully and saw that he should be leaving the Army in less than thirty days. If I filed charges against him, his departure would be delayed, and if he was found guilty of desertion, as he most certainly would be, then his discharge would be delayed until he had served out his sentence. It seemed to me that the best thing for the Army would be to get rid of this young man once and for all, so I decided to forget the court-marshal charges and sign his discharge papers.

As I looked over the papers, I came to a section that required me to check one of two boxes. One box was labeled "honorable discharge" and the other was labeled "dishonorable discharge." I thought about how much difficulty Danny had caused for me and everyone else. It seemed to me that he should not get off scot-free. After pondering the matter a little more I checked the dishonorable box.

A couple of days later, the First Sergeant came into my office with some papers in his hand. With a very serious look on his face he said, "These are orders that just came in from DC that award Danny the Silver Star. You cannot give him a dishonorable discharge." I looked at the papers and said, "You're right, bring me his discharge," and I changed the dishonorable to honorable. The Silver Star is the third highest medal, behind the Congressional Medal of Honor and the Distinguished Service Cross, which is awarded by the U.S. Government for valor in combat. I don't remember now what he had done to earn it, but Danny had done something very heroic in Vietnam.

Danny was a certified hero. At some point he had shown great courage in battle in Vietnam, and if he is still alive today, he has a medal and Presidential Citation to prove it.

It may have been for only a few minutes, but he had performed some act of bravery that had earned him this considerable honor. I do not know what had happened to him to turn him into a misfit when he returned to the United States. We did not know about Post Traumatic Stress Disorder (PTSD) then, but perhaps whatever he had done in Vietnam had haunted him, and he was compelled to try to dull the remembrance of it with alcohol and bad behavior. Whatever the reason, in Vietnam he had been a great success, a hero, if only for a short time, but in the battle of everyday existence here in the United States he had proved to be a failure.

SFC MACK RICE

Sergeant First Class Mack F. Rice was my light weapons expert on Mobile Advisory Team 66 in Vietnam. He performed his duties well while under my command. He was young, though not as young as I, and was serving his second tour in country (Vietnam). If I had a choice, I usually took him with me on difficult assignments because I felt that he was my best man. One of those difficult assignments was a sweep with elements of two South Vietnamese companies across the Cambodian boarder into enemy territory.

One afternoon my Vietnamese counterpart, Captain Tail, came to me and said that he would like for us to go into Province Headquarters in the morning to meet with his S3 operations officer, Major Trang, and with our U.S. S3 operations officer, Major Barton, to discuss a proposed operation. In the morning we flew together on the supply chopper to headquarters.

We went to Major Trang's office where Major Barton soon joined us. After exchanging salutes and handshakes, we all sat down around a large map of the province that was spread out on a table. The Vietnamese S3, who spoke a fair amount of English, pointed to a spot just inside the Cambodian border and said that the VC had set up a base camp there. He wanted Tail to take elements of two companies into this area and burn the structures that had been built there by the VC. He expected that the VC would run, but if not, we should kill as many as possible.

The plan seemed simple, and I agreed to the strategy. Major Barton said that he and Major Trang would monitor the operation from a helicopter circling above. I wondered if the Cambodian government knew we were going into their country. I suspected that they did not. I decided not to ask because I figured it was not my problem, and it wouldn't change anything. I was in favor of going after the VC wherever they were if it would make our sector more secure.

The day before the operation, we received our orders by code over the radio. When I plotted our route of travel, I saw that it showed us being dropped next to the border by helicopters, but it did not show us going across. I told Mack that I wanted him to go with me. He reminded me that it wasn't his turn, but I told him that this was a special operation and that I needed him. He nodded his head, indicating that he understood, and accepted the assignment without complaint. I began to realize that I depended on Mack quite a bit. He was young and strong, and he had a considerable amount of valuable experience.

The next morning, October 22, we arose and had our breakfast as usual. Mack got up from the table and went out into the courtyard. He immediately came back with a very worried look on his face. "This is going to be a terrible operation," he said. "The Vietnamese soldiers are armed to the hilt, and their women are standing around crying and telling them good-bye like they are not coming back."

I grabbed my gear and went outside to find it just as Mack had described. I had never seen our troops so well prepared before. They had machine guns and LAWs (light antitank weapons) and they were all wearing boots and helmets. Mack came back out wearing a flak jacket, which was quite a statement on what was bound to be a very warm and humid day.

The day started badly. As we all stood around in the courtyard, preparing and adjusting our gear, one of the Vietnamese soldiers I knew was standing next to me. He was carrying a LAW, which is an antitank weapon that looks like a collapsible tube. When opened and extended, it becomes armed. It has adjustable sights and is fired by pushing a button. It is disposable, and once fired, you merely throw away the tube. It fires a very powerful rocket that is capable of penetrating armor or fortified positions. It is a light and very portable alternative to carrying a recoilless rifle (bazooka).

The soldier removed the LAW from his shoulder and set it down on the base of a concrete monument that was in front of him. As the LAW touched the concrete, it unexpectedly fired, making a loud noise and pulverizing the face of the soldier. He was only about six feet from where I was standing. Miraculously I was not hit, only slightly stunned by the explosion. I immediately went to him, kneeled down, and examined his wounds. I don't know if he was hit with pieces of the rocket or pieces of cement, or both. His face was a mess, but he was still alive.

I ran to the radio inside our bunker and called for a dust-off helicopter, while his compatriots bandaged his wounds as best they could. The chopper got there really fast, and a few minutes after it departed, the medic on board called back to say that the man would probably live but was sure to lose both eyes. Prior to this accident, the young man was probably the most handsome man in the entire Ben Cau force. I never saw him again.

After we got the injured man out, we all walked into a nearby field and loaded into choppers for the short flight out to the border. It was the largest airlift in which I had ever participated. There were several choppers, carrying about eighty men in three lifts. Dai uy Tail, Mack, and I rode in the same chopper. As we landed, I immediately heard the sounds of battle.

We were coming into a hot landing zone (LZ). There was a small compound of six or seven wooden buildings to the west just across the border, and our men were receiving small-arms fire from it. I saw two VC soldiers come out of their compound and begin to fire a machine gun at our people. Soon, mortar rounds began to fall randomly in the field where we were spread out. I watched through binoculars as our people moved to the left and attacked the nearest building. They took the building quickly, and soon it was burning from their torches.

Major Barton came over the radio and said that he and Major Trang, the Vietnamese S3, were on station above. I gave him a report on what was happening below and said I would keep him advised. The mortar rounds began to fall fairly regularly, and I estimated that the enemy must have been firing two or possibly three tubes at us.

As we moved closer to the action, the VC small-arms and machine-gun fire also began to come our way. We were standing in the open with no cover to get behind, and it became very uncomfortable as bullet rounds began to kick up the dirt around us. We were between 300 and 400 meters from the VC machine gun, but, fortunately for us, the Vietnamese on both sides were notoriously bad shots. Most of the rounds fell short or wide of our position. After only a short time, there was another building smoking as our people put a torch to it.

A few minutes after the second building began to burn, two of our men were brought to us with serious wounds. Both had head and neck wounds and needed immediate attention. One had a large bandage over his forehead and eyes, indicating possible eye and face damage. I immediately called for a medical chopper to evacuate the wounded. Mortar rounds continued to fall around us, some very close, and the VCs on the machine gun continued to fire at our people who were nearest to the village.

After only a few minutes, the pilot of the medevac came over the radio and asked me to throw smoke to mark our position. Captain Tail was standing next to me, and I asked him to have one of his people throw smoke. Instead of throwing the smoke grenade, he handed it to me and backed away. I pulled the ring and threw out the grenade, which was red smoke.

It was standard procedure to throw the grenade and then ask the chopper pilot to identify the color. The VC would sometimes listen in on our frequency, and when they heard us say we were throwing smoke, they would also throw out a smoke grenade, trying to lure the chopper to their position so they could shoot it down.

On this day when we were standing next to the Cambodian boarder, the smoke grenade that Captain Tail had handed me proved to be red when I threw it. The chopper pilot identified the smoke correctly and said that he was coming in. I suddenly realized that Tail and his men were running away from us as the VC concentrated their fire on the helicopter and on the red smoke grenade I had just thrown. In addition to the mortars, the enemy small arms and the machine gun began to also rake our position with fire. As the chopper landed, it kicked up a lot of dust that mixed with the smoke and debris from the mortar rounds that were impacting on our position. The combination of dust, smoke, and noise from the chopper and the mortars created a frightening scene that caused all of the Vietnamese soldiers around us to scatter.

Mack and my radio operator helped the two wounded soldiers onto the chopper as mortar rounds fell dangerously close. There was no cover because we were standing in an open field. I reported the situation to Major Barton over the radio, and he informed me that he had already called for gunship helicopters, which were on station above us. I asked Mack to give me a distance and direction to the machine gun. Despite the numerous bullet rounds and mortar explosions impacting around us, he pulled out his compass and map and made the calculations.

In a very short time, the gunship pilot came over the radio. "This is Red Dog above you. What can we do?"

Before departing, Tail had given me coordinates of where his men thought the VC mortar crews were located. Mack gave me his estimate of the direction and distance to the machine gun. "Red Dog," I said, "this is Sassy Cat Six. I want you to shoot up the following targets."

I gave him the coordinates. After a short pause, Red Dog came back over the radio. "Sorry, Sassy Cat. No can do. That target is in Cambodia."

I was astonished at the response. "Do you mean to tell me that they sent us in here and did not give you permission to shoot into Cambodia?"

The answer was, "That's a roger, Sassy Cat. Sorry."

At about this time I was vaguely aware that someone was calling my name in a very loud and agitated voice. I looked up to see Mack standing a few feet away, yelling at the top of his voice, telling me that our Vietnamese counterparts had completely left the field. We were facing the enemy alone. I looked at my radio operator, who now had a look of terror on his face, as deafening explosions erupted all around us.

My first inclination was to run and catch up with the others because I had a vision of being captured, which I thought would be worse than being killed. But instead of running, I decided to stay. I resolved that I would not leave until we had finished our mission and inflicted whatever damage we could on the enemy. I knew that this VC unit had come to our village many times dropping mortars on us, killing or wounding soldiers and civilians alike. They had come into our village at night, intimidated our people, and exhorted them to kill us in our sleep. They had moved with impunity across this border to attack, assassinate, and terrorize on our side, and then had been able to return to safety across this imaginary line, merely a black line drawn on a map. Now they were doing it again, and our troops did not have the gumption to confront them. I had had enough. We were finally in the enemy's backyard, and I hated to leave until we had done him some damage. Besides it would have been very dangerous to try to run across the large empty field with the VC shooting at us. We had to get some fire on the enemy in order to cover our withdrawal, and it was obvious our South Vietnamese friends were not going to be around to help us. I felt that I had to call a fire mission on the enemy, but I needed Mack to help me. The situation was so dangerous that I did not feel that I could order him to stay.

"Mack," I yelled, trying to carry my voice above the din of the exploding mortar rounds, "I can't leave until I have called a fire mission on the enemy. Will you stay with me?" He considered the question for just a moment and then the look on his face turned from one of concern to one of resolve. "I'll stay," he said as a mortar round landed behind him shaking the ground where we stood.

I then turned my attention back to the gunship circling above us. I had to yell into the radio mike in order to be heard above the roar of the exploding mortar rounds. "Red Dog," I yelled, "this is Sassy Cat Six," emphasizing the "six," meaning the caller was a commander. He didn't know that I was only a first lieutenant. "I'm the commander of this operation, and I'm telling you that this is Vietnam, not Cambodia. I want you to shoot up that target and anything else you see that looks like the bad guys."

It was a very improbable assertion since everyone knew it was not Vietnam, but I realized that I couldn't order him to shoot into Cambodia. In fact, there was probably no one in the whole province who could order him to shoot into Cambodia, so the only thing I could do was to advocate for it being Vietnam.

After a long pause, "Roger," was the response. "This is Red Dog, and I am attacking this target based on your order, and I note that your call sign is Sassy Cat Six."

Almost immediately, the chopper unleashed a horrendous volume of firepower from rockets onto the machine gun emplacement on the other side of the border. It was completely knocked out. The enemy compound was totally unfortified since the enemy had never before needed to worry about being attacked in their sanctuary.

At about this time, Major Barton came over the radio and asked me to relay a message to Captain Tail. I responded that I couldn't relay a message because Tail wasn't there. "You should never be separated from your counterpart," he said.

I didn't know how to respond. I didn't want to tell him that Tail ran off while Mack and I were taking care of his wounded men, so I said, "During that last mortar barrage, it was necessary for us to go in separate directions."

After a pause, Major Barton answered, "OK, just tell him to call his S3 when you catch up with him."

I then gave Red Dog the suspected coordinates of the VC mortar crew. After a couple of passes and more rocket fire from the chopper, there was a secondary explosion, leading me to think we had knocked out at least one of the mortars. Red Dog came over the radio, saying, "I have people on the ground, running. Shall I fire?"

"What direction are they running in?" I asked.

"West," was the answer.

I figured that they were the rest of the VC who had been with the machine gun. I said, "Roger, Red Dog. Go ahead." Another burst of fire erupted from the ship, but I couldn't tell the result.

At about this time, Mack insisted that we pull out before it was too late. Because I had been absorbed with the fire missions over the radio, I hadn't noticed that our RF troops were now completely on the other side of the large field, almost out of sight. While I had been working the gunship over the radio, Mack and my radio operator had been standing there watching the mortar rounds fall, knowing that at any moment the next one might fall on us. Mack had stood firm when the others had run. He had carried the wounded to the helicopter and had lifted them aboard while we had been under intense fire. He had risked his life to do his duty, and, although I didn't know it at the time, he would do it again before the day was done. Now, he wisely knew that it was time for us to get out while we still could.

We began to run as fast as we could to catch up to the RF soldiers. When we reached the other side of the field, we found Captain Tail and his troops resting under a border of small trees. There were two more very seriously wounded soldiers there, and once again I called for a dust-off. As the chopper came into view,

Tail pleaded, "No more smoke. Use this." He held up the backside of his map, which made a nice white panel.

I picked up the radio mike and said, "Dust-off, we cannot throw smoke because it draws fire."

"Never mind," he said, "I see your panel." Whereupon he dropped down to about fifteen feet off the ground and came directly toward us. The enemy apparently saw him also and began lobbing mortars at him, which fell around us as well.

Captain Tail and his troops scattered again, leaving Mack and me to load their two wounded soldiers. Mortar rounds fell around the chopper and us. Mack carried one man and I carried the other to the chopper. As we helped them aboard, one round of mortar landed directly on the other side of the chopper. I heard the distinct sound of metal hitting against metal as the shrapnel dug into the body of the aircraft. How we escaped being hit, I do not know.

Once the helicopter had lifted off the ground, I got back on the radio. "Red Dog," I said, "This is Sassy Cat Six. I need some more ordnance." I gave him the general vicinity of where I thought the fire was coming from. By now Red Dog was happy to shoot anywhere we wanted, assuming the blame would fall on me if there were any repercussions. Shortly, the incoming mortar rounds slackened, and Mack and I had to once again run in order to catch up with our troops. They had had enough of this mini Cambodian invasion and were heading for home.

I didn't know if Captain Tail had received permission from his commander to withdraw or not. I never knew how many of the enemy there were, but I suspected there were quite a few, including enough mortar crews to keep rounds pouring down on us constantly.

By the time the last mortar round fell, it was almost 1200 hours and we had been in combat all morning. Captain Tail estimated that the enemy had fired approximately 120 rounds of mortar at us over the course of the morning.

As a result of his heroic actions, SFC Mack Rice was recommended for the Bronze Star with V for valor. I wrote an eyewitness report of his actions and signed his recommendation. When I left Vietnam at the end of January I did not know whether he had received the award or not.

In the spring of 2005, while doing research at the National Archives in Maryland, I found a copy of his approved citation for the Bronze star with V for his actions that day in Cambodia. I resolved then to try to find him when I returned home to Raleigh. About a week later, I found him using a professional search company that advertised, "Find your old military buddies." I called the telephone number they had given me, and left a voicemail for him to give me a call back if he was the same Mack Rice that I had known in Vietnam. He called back and we had a great conversation. I congratulated him on receiving the Bronze Star with V and said, "Mack, I always thought you were my best man and that is why I usually took you on the tough operations." He laughed and said "Well, I did notice that you took me on the tough ones."

That conversation reminded me of another incident that had happened after the Cambodian incursion. We were stationed in another village near Tay Ninh City. We knew that the VC were active in this village and we had encouraged the Vietnamese lieutenant who commanded our little outpost to send out night ambushes to disrupt the enemy movement and free the village from intimidation. He took our advice and began sending out ambush patrols at night around the village. One night the lieutenant came into our bunker at about midnight, awoke us and said that his ambush patrol had fired on an enemy unit, and was in a firefight. He needed to take out a relief force to assist his men and bring them back safely.

I could tell that the lieutenant wanted me to come with him so I told him that I would join him as soon as I could get dressed. I got out of bed, put on my clothes, and sat back down on the edge of my bunk to put on my boots. As I looked down to lace up the boots, I was thinking that I would tell Mack to come with me. When I looked up he was already sitting on the edge of his bunk putting on his boots. Without my having to speak at all he said, "I'll come with you." Mack was a hero, the kind of hero who is there for the long run. He retired from the U.S. Army as a Command Sergeant Major, the highest rank that an enlisted man can achieve.

YOGI YARBOROUGH

The other hero I would like to describe never served in the military. He was a short stocky man named Yogi Yarborough. He was given the name Yogi by a baseball scout who said that he reminded him of Yogi Berra. Unfortunately Yogi's chances to play professional baseball were cut short by a back injury, but as he was prone to do throughout his life, he ignored the setback and proceeded to graduate from High Point College, went into the furniture hardware business, and became a self-made millionaire.

In Yogi's case the term "self-made" takes on new meaning. The tenth of eleven children born to a small Davidson County tobacco farmer, Yogi literally made himself into an extraordinarily successful man. He told me that he started his hardware business with $10,000 he had saved as a salesman plus a $10,000 loan he obtained from a sympathetic local banker. At first, he was a one-man show, acting as the company's president and only salesman. When out on the road selling, he slept in his car and shaved in gas station restrooms in order to save money. In less than five years he turned his small business into a multimillion dollar company. But his financial and business success was not what really made him exceptional. It was his extraordinary service to God and his fellow men that made him a real hero.

He was a hero for the long run like Mack Rice, not a short run hero. As you might expect he was a civic leader in his hometown of High Point, NC, doing yeoman's service for Hospice of the Piedmont, The Rotary Club, Mobile Meals, the High Point Community Foundation, and several other organizations. He was a strong supporter of his church and a loving family man. His greatest asset, however, was his love of people. He counted as his "friends" more people than any person I have ever known. People from all walks of life and all stations in society claimed him as their friend, and he always took time to speak to them and listen to them and help them with their problems if he could.

I was happy to be one of Yogi's friends. After I moved from High Point to Raleigh in 1985, we had less contact and I lost track of Yogi. One day in 2004 he called me and said that he was coming to visit. He came to Raleigh and we had lunch at a local restaurant. As we walked from my office to his car I noticed that he had a slight limp in his left leg, so I asked him about it. He said that the doctors were running tests and thought it might be Lou Gehrig's Disease (ALS), but he was not worried about it, that it was in God's hands anyway. A couple of months later, I heard through a mutual friend that it was Lou Gehrig's, and called him about it. Still upbeat, he said that he intended to live with the disease, keep on doing what he could do, and not worry about it.

Several months later I was in High Point and stopped at his house to see him. I was alarmed at how fast the disease was attacking his body. He was not able to walk except with a walker and then with great difficulty, and his speech was quite slurred. He had a male nurse there who helped him get around. He introduced me to the man and called him, "my friend Raymond." Yogi and I had a long talk and the whole time we talked he remained upbeat, expressing more concern for others than himself, and said, "I try to focus on what I can do, as opposed to what I can't do." After an hour or so he said that he was sorry to say that he had to leave to go to a luncheon meeting down town with a local civic leader. I just stood there in his driveway and watched with admiration as he gamely struggled, with Raymond's help, across his driveway to his car and drove off to his meeting.

Before he died at the young age of sixty-five, some people in High Point held a dinner in his honor with some of his closest friends. They had to limit attendance to 500 people because of a lack of space, and it was said that there were many more of "his friends" who wanted to attend but were not able.

The local newspaper did a story on Yogi a few months before his death. The reporter started the interview with the question, "Do you ever ask, 'why me?'" Yogi's answer was, "I would never ask that question, and I wouldn't ask for a miracle…God knows the condition I'm in, and God loves me and I know He'll give me the strength to deal with whatever I have to deal with." Yes, Yogi was a hero for the long run, and we would all do well to model our lives after him.

WE NEED ALL OF OUR HEROES

We have looked at three very different men who were three very different types of hero. We need all three of them. We need the man or woman who will risk everything and take extraordinary risk to accomplish a task. The military especially needs this kind of hero who will do extraordinary things in combat. These heroes will take out the machine gun or the mortar crew that is causing large numbers of casualties on our side. They will crawl out under fire and bring back a wounded buddy. They will show extraordinary courage for brief periods of time that will win the day in battle, and permit the rest of us to do our duty. They will generally perform these acts of valor over relatively short periods of time, usually a day or less, maybe in just a few minutes. They are the heroes for the short run, and we need them when only raw courage can save the day.

The heroes that I have called heroes for the long term will also perform daring acts of valor, but they are with us for the long pull. They are people like Mack Rice, who are the backbone of our military, without whom we could accomplish nothing.

People like Yogi Yarborough are the kind of heroes who are the backbone of our nation. They are the selfless public servants, clergymen and clergywomen, missionaries, shelter operators, medical workers, and volunteers of all sorts. They are our lighthouses in the storm, our strength in times of trial, and our comforters in times of trouble. They are God's angels on earth doing God's work.

HEROES FROM THE BIBLE

The Holy Bible is full of courageous people. The Old Testament, in particular, gives us accounts of many mighty warriors who were very courageous. The quote that appears at the start of this chapter is from the Book of Joshua, and it is God's words spoken to Joshua in order to give him the courage to take the people of Israel across the River Jordan into the Promised Land. The problem was that this land, which had been bequeathed to Moses and the Israelites, was not vacant. It was inhabited by fierce, warlike people who would not relish having this foreign tribe move into their territory. Joshua knew that they would fight and he was probably hesitant to take up the challenge.

God said to him, "Have I not commanded you; 'Be strong and courageous. Do not be terrified; do not be discouraged, for the Lord your God will be with you wherever you go.'" (Joshua 1:9). Notice that it is a command, not a request. God does not give us a choice in the matter. When he wants us to do something, he gives us a command not a suggestion. Interestingly, many U.S. soldiers in Iraq now wear a dog-tag sized shield with this biblical quote stamped upon it. For this reason it has been labeled the Soldiers Creed. Reportedly many of the men gather to pray in the morning before they go out on operation, and they repeat this creed as part of their prayers.

The most famous warrior hero in the Bible is David, and the most famous story about his courage is his battle against the giant Goliath. When he faces Goliath on the battlefield he says, "You come against me with sword and spear and javelin, but I come against you in the name of the Lord Almighty." Of course, as every child in Sunday school knows, David defeats the giant and the Israelis are inspired by him to defeat the entire Philistine army.

There are many more warrior heroes in the Old Testament to include Samson, Jehu, Abner, Jehoshaphat, and Gideon. The New Testament, however, introduces us to a new type of hero. Jesus' disciples become men of courage after the resurrection, but prior to this they were anything but heroes. The Gospels describe them as fearful, tentative and a bit dull. When the Temple guards apprehend Jesus, Peter, the most vocal and enthusiastic of the disciples, draws his sword to defend the Lord, but later he becomes fearful and renounces Jesus three times. When we see these men again after the resurrection and after they have received the Holy Sprit, they have become transformed indeed. They become men of courage who are filled with the Spirit and with knowledge beyond their education. This transformation is strong evidence for the truth of the resurrection. What else could explain such a transformation of people from being ordinary to becoming extraordinary human beings?

In the Book of Acts, the transformed disciples go about teaching the word of God, as revealed to them by Christ, with great conviction and boldness. Even their detractors, the Sadducees, say they are astonished at the change. Acts 3:13 says, "When they saw the courage of Peter and John and realized that they were unschooled, ordinary men, they were astonished and they took note that these men had been with Jesus." After the resurrection, all of the disciples seem to acquire this God-given courage and boldness that caused them to proclaim the truth of Christ until their deaths, which they also faced boldly.

The apostle Paul is himself a paragon of courage. This first-century hero traveled all over the Roman Empire spreading the Gospel, enduring great risk and discomfort. He was repeatedly imprisoned and beaten and on one occasion stoned almost to death. Finally, we are told that the Lord spoke to him and said, "Take courage! As you have testified about me in Jerusalem, so you must testify in Rome." Dutifully, he goes to Rome where he is imprisoned and presumably eventually executed by the Romans.

I have come to realize that the most courageous individual in the Bible is Jesus Christ . This may come as a surprise to some people. In our modern Christian Church we have come to think of Jesus as more than a mere man, as we should, but at the same time we have often characterized him as less than a man as well. Some, who don't know him, would describe him as an effete pacifist who angered the authorities and faced an untimely death by execution. Nothing could be further from the truth. Jesus was not an elite intellectual flitting about teaching love and peace.

Prior to starting his ministry at the age of around thirty, he most likely worked at his earthly father's trade of carpentry. Even today this is a very physically demanding job, and it was probably more so in the first century. Most likely then, Jesus was physically strong and rugged. When he started his ministry, he and his disciples walked all over Palestine, a very taxing way to travel, requiring stamina and strength. Although he was a carpenter he was certainly not ignorant. He could read and write, and the Gospels describe him as taking part in many intellectual discussions with the most educated men of his day. We also learn from these verbal exchanges, that he was cunning and had a powerful command of the spoken word. More significantly, we learn from these discourses that he was very courageous.

As Jesus went about teaching, the religious and political leaders in Palestine were constantly challenging him and trying to catch him in statements that could be considered blasphemy, an offense carrying the penalty of death. He knew this and yet he continued to challenge them knowing that it would eventually mean his death, for this was a time when human life was cheap, and those who ruled maintained their power through ruthless means, including dispatching their opponents in great numbers if need be. It took considerable courage to continue to challenge the authorities in this way. Additionally, because he seemed to have certain divine knowledge of the future, he knew when he set out on his final trip to Jerusalem, that he faced a certain and horrible death on the cross. Despite this knowledge, he chose to make this journey towards his inevitable death.

In a tight situation we always think we are going to make it. In an old movie from the 1970's Steve McQueen played a U.S. sailor who was struggling to save some innocent people who were caught in the crossfire as Japan invaded China before the Second World War. At the end of the movie, he had moved all of his people to safety, but he is the last one out, and he has to run across an open courtyard to safety. As he runs he is fatally shot and falls to the ground. Lying there dying, his last words are, "I thought I was going to make it." I remember thinking the same thing, that he was going to make it, and it was a real shock when he does not. Aren't we all like that? No matter how bad the situation or no matter how low the odds, we think that we are going to make it. But Jesus knew that he would not survive the trip, and he went anyway in order to save our souls. That is courage of the highest order. "Greater love has no one than this, that he lay down his life for his friends" (John 15:13). We are those friends. With a sacrifice greater than that of Congressional Medal of Honor holders who fell on hand grenades in order to save their buddies, Jesus gave his life for us in the eternal battle for souls.

These biblical heroes, from both the Old and the New Testaments, were empowered with courage and abilities beyond their natural conditions. Their power and their courage came from God. None of them, except for Jesus, seem to have been born with it. God bestowed their courage upon them, and this is where we must also look for the courage that we need to face the trials and the challenges in our lives. Like the soldiers in Iraq who wear the little shields engraved with the Soldier's Creed, we must turn to him for our strength and our courage. When we are discouraged and afraid we must remember the words of the Psalmist, "I will say of the Lord 'he is my refuge and my fortress, my God, in whom I trust.'" (Psalm 91:2). The only courage that counts is the courage that comes from God. Anything else is merely foolhardiness.

SIX

The Imposter

I have come that they may have life,
and have it to the full.

—John 10:10

For about thirty days during the fall of 1969, a U.S. Army rifle company was stationed just outside of the village of Ben Cau. Our MAT 66 team was there also for a second stay, having completed our assignment at Tra Vo. The rifle company was commanded by a young redheaded American Captain who had graduated from the Citadel and was an excellent military leader. I don't remember his name but will call him Captain "Red." His company was part of the U.S. Army's belated attempt at Vietnamization.

One day Captain "Red" came by our bunker and invited me to go up the river by boat with him to Tay Ninh City, and since it sounded like a good adventure, I agreed. When we arrived at the shore, I was surprised to see a small sixteen-foot aluminum boat with an outboard motor. I guess I was expecting something larger, such as, a navy PT boat, and I must admit that I was a bit concerned. Nevertheless, I stepped aboard with "Red" and four of his enlisted men. I noticed that his first sergeant was not along; assuming that he, too, thought it was not a very wise mode of travel.

The trip up the river was very pleasant. It was a fair day and the wind created by the motion of the boat was cooling. It reminded me of carefree, lazy days as a boy on the York River back home in Virginia. The river was fairly wide and we motored up the middle, which I felt gave us some welcomed distance from possible snipers along the shore. We arrived at the dock at Tay Ninh about midday. There was a large market situated there, which was full of merchandise, produce, and people. The hustle and bustle of the market presented a feeling of normal commerce, which made thoughts of the war seem out of place and far off. I had arranged for our jeep to be waiting, and we all went in separate directions with an understanding that we would meet back at the dock at 1500 hours for the return trip back to Ben Cau. I went to province headquarters and to the PX (post exchange) but couldn't buy much because of the limited carrying capacity of the boat.

At the appointed hour, I arrived back at the dock to find the others already waiting. We all knew that it was important to get back well before dark because Charlie basically ruled the night. Plus anything moving at night was potentially fair game for our aircraft to fire upon. The trip back started out as pleasantly as before, but I felt more uneasy, knowing that anytime we traveled out to somewhere in the morning, the enemy might be waiting for our return that afternoon along the same route. As we motored down the river, we all fixed our eyes on the shoreline with our rifles at the ready. I watched the shore to our right.

After we had been traveling approximately thirty minutes, staying to the middle of the river, I spied movement in the water next to the shore about 200 meters away. After a few seconds of watching the moving object intently, I was able to identify it as a man who appeared to be in the water near the shore with his shoulders and head visible. His right arm was extended straight up, and he appeared to be waving at us. I immediately tapped Captain "Red" on the shoulder and pointed at the man in the river. "Red" motioned the driver of the boat to head toward him.

As we drew closer to the shore, all sorts of thoughts went though my head. I could tell that he was a young Vietnamese man with medium-length black hair. I wondered if it was a trick, a ploy to get us closer to the shore so that his buddies could fire on us with rifles and rocket launchers. Or was it someone in trouble, perhaps a fisherman or a civilian who was injured and needed help? As we got closer, I became certain it was trouble and raised my rifle in readiness.

When we got within thirty or forty feet of the man, the situation became clear. The young man was dead. His eyes were open but rolled back in his head. He had apparently died with his right arm outstretched, frozen in an extended position. As the waves from the river lapped against the shore, he swayed back and forth so that he appeared to be waving his arm. As the pilot pulled the boat away to continue down the river, I turned and watched him floating there, waving good-bye as we moved away. He seemed to be staring at us as if he had something he wanted to say from the grave, perhaps something like, "You had better be careful. I didn't think I would end up like this, and it could happen to you."

I assume this man was a dead VC, probably killed in some battle, perhaps in the night ambush we had sprung just a few weeks before. He had been left to float aimlessly up and down the river. In my own mind, I dubbed him "the imposter" because he was obviously dead but seemed to be pretending to be alive. There were dead bodies like that scattered all over Vietnam. Sometimes the peasants would bury them, as they had after our ambush, but often they would just leave their dead where they fell, as evidenced by the fact that we occasionally found human skeletons in the jungle while out on patrol. We continued down the river without further incident and arrived back home in Ben Cau safely. When I close my eyes and think about it, I can still see "the imposter's" face.

THE FALSE SELF

Sometimes "the imposter's" face will flash across my mind, and I wonder why is this macabre character visiting me now after all of these years? I have come to see it as a warning that I am encountering a situation in myself or in another person where the "poser" is taking over. These are times when I find that I am not acting like the person that I really am, the person that God meant me to be. We can call this other self the "poser," and if we are not careful he can take over the "real" person.

In his book *Wild at Heart*, John Eldridge calls this other person the "False Self." He says that it is the persona we assume in order to hide the hurts, he calls them wounds, which we have received in the past while living our real lives. He says that men are particularly susceptible to doing this because of the pressures that are put on us to perform as men, to be manly, to show no emotion, to always be competent and self assured. The "false self" allows us to avoid the otherwise painful aspects of our real lives. For many men this "false self" leaves us as mechanical beings with no feelings and no realization of who we really are.

When I was in Vietnam I shut down my feelings as a means of self-protection. I remember the first time that I was among people who were wounded and dying. I called for a medical evacuation by helicopter, and then I walked among the wounded while we waited for the choppers to come. I saw the look of fear and anguish in their eyes and I felt great compassion for them. I knelt down over one man who had a mangled leg. I touched the bandage that inadequately covered his wound as though I could heal him, but of course I could not, and he wrenched with pain at my touch. After that day, I suppressed my feelings for the injured. Actually, I ceased to feel anything. It was a false face that I wore for many years after, a face that I sometimes still struggle to throw off.

Many men strive to present a face that is not real. We try too hard to be macho, or manly, or ruthless, or nonchalant, or sophisticated, or whatever it is that we think our little corner of the world demands. Women are not immune from this tendency to be posers as well. With more and more women moving into business, assuming their roles as managers and "movers and shakers," there is a strong tendency to forsake their womanhood and take on manly ways. God's plan for us is to be who he made us to be, and we all know in our hearts who that person is. George Eliot said, "It is never too late to be what you might have been." We are all able to recognize when we stray into the role of the poser, even if we don't have the face of the "imposter" burned into our subconscious.

GOD WANTS US TO BE FULLY ALIVE

The other impression that the "imposter" has made on me is that many of us exist, but we are not truly alive; that is, we are not living the full lives that God intended. When I first saw the "imposter," I thought that he was alive. I thought that he was a real person in the water who was moving and waving his hand, trying to get our attention. Upon closer examination I discovered that he was not alive at all, but merely seemed to be alive. Unfortunately, many of us are also pretending to be living real lives but we are not.

Emerson said that many of us live "lives of quiet desperation." We go about our daily existence, but are we really living? Our very society is drowning in shallow self-absorption, where many people merely go from one obsession to the next, from one addiction to the next, from one disappointing marriage to the next, from one unfulfilling career to the next. We have our toys, our drugs, our TVs, and our one-night stands, but do we really have life as it was meant to be? Many people report that their lives are empty, that they are only surviving, that there is no meaning in their lives. Jesus said that he came to bring us life, and that he wants us to have the fullest life possible. The Apostle Paul said, "The hour has come for you to wake up from your slumber, because our salvation is nearer now than when we first believed. The night is nearly over; the day is almost here. So let us put aside the deeds of darkness and put on the armor of light. Let us behave decently, as in the daytime, not in orgies and drunkenness, not in sexual immorality and debauchery, not in dissension and jealousy" (Romans 13:11–13). As Paul says we need to wake up and begin to live a real life, the one that we were meant to live.

Even some Christians seem to be missing out on this message. Once I was in a Christian bookstore when I bumped into a man I knew casually. He inquired if I was a Christian, and I happily answered "yes." Then he said in a very serious tone, "I just can't wait until the rapture comes." I was a bit taken back and didn't know exactly how to respond. While I was struggling for words, his wife grabbed his arm and pulled him away. After he left, I thought a lot about his statement. I didn't know him well, but I wondered if he was actually just biding time here waiting for the end times. I had never thought the end of the world as being something I should long for to come quickly. I had always thought of it as something far off that I did not actually have to think much about. I am looking forward to seeing Jesus, and the Bible tells me it will happen when I die. Jesus says to the thief on the cross, "I tell you the truth, today you will be with me in paradise" (Luke 23:43). Some Christians talk like they merely exist here on earth, longing for the end.

St. Irenaeus said, "The glory of God is man fully alive." Christians, more than anyone, should live lives that are fully alive. When Jesus promised us eternal life, he was referring to a life that begins here and now and extends into the future, and eventually into eternity (Luke 18:29–30). He said, "I am the Bread of life" (John 6:48). The Gospel writer John says, "In him was life, and that life was the light of men" (John 1:4). Jesus did not say, "Life is hard and then you die, but then you will have salvation." Life may be hard at times, maybe a great deal of the time for some of us, but it should not be just a time of waiting. It should be a time of being "fully alive" in fellowship with our God and other Christians.

The Psalmist wrote, "I will see the goodness of the Lord in the land of the living" (Ps. 27:13). God put us here in the land of the living for a purpose. It is up to us to discern that purpose and live in such a way as to fulfill all that he has in store for us. The "impostor" is proof that life is short and must not be wasted, and likewise he warns us with the wave of his arm against living in any way that does not glorify God and does not allow us to assume our proper roles as Kingdom dwellers.

SEVEN

The Third Wake-up Call

Even though I walk through the valley of the shadow of death,
I will fear no evil, for you are with me;

—Psalm 23:4

Since Ben Cau was located in a very remote part of Tay Ninh Province and the roads were not secure, at least one member of our team went into province headquarters every week. It was an opportunity for one of us to pick up some supplies and experience a little bit of rest and recuperation, if only for a short while. One morning, a week or so prior to the completion of our second tour at Ben Cau, I found myself on the work chopper with the supply sergeant, SFC Wallace, and two American first lieutenants, who were stationed with a mobile advisory team in a remote outpost in the sector north of us called War Zone C. One of the officers was black, the other white, and it was obvious they were good friends and enjoyed working together. The flight to Tay Ninh was short, and we soon found ourselves walking across the runway, comparing notes about what we needed to do and what time we would need to be back at the airstrip for the flight back. It was agreed that we would meet at the NCO Club when we were finished with our work.

I really didn't have much to do except to pick up our mail and a case of beer. I was looking forward mostly to having a relaxing mixed drink back at the air-conditioned NCO Club. These trips to headquarters were like a brief return to civilization, and it was a nice respite from the rugged life back at Ben Cau.

Thirty minutes before our agreed departure time, I went to the NCO Club and sat down at the bar. After considering my choices of mixed drinks, I ordered a tall, cool gin and tonic packed full of ice. As I took my first couple of delightful sips from the drink, I saw the two lieutenants and Sergeant Wallace come into the bar. They were finished with their business and anxious to get back on the chopper, which they said, was on the airstrip ready to go. I suggested they sit down and join me for a drink, but they would have nothing of it. The supply sergeant told me that another chopper would be leaving in about thirty minutes to deliver a barrel of gasoline to another outpost, and I could wait and catch that one back to Ben Cau. Looking at that cool drink sitting in front of me, I readily agreed.

After finishing the drink, I went out to the airstrip and found the second chopper with a fifty-five-gallon drum of gasoline sitting next to it. I helped the door gunner and the pilot load the gas, which I remember as being very heavy, and we took off for Ben Cau. The flight was short, and upon landing, I walked into our bunker where I found everyone sitting around, listening to our command radio. They all looked up and stared at me as though they had seen a ghost.

"What's going on?" I asked.

Mack spoke up and said in an excited tone of voice, "The supply chopper went down, and we thought you were on it!"

I glanced at Dave, who gave me a quick stare and looked away, saying, "We thought you had gone and gotten yourself killed just when we were getting used to you."

"What about the two lieutenants and the supply sergeant?" I asked.

"It sounds like they're all dead," someone said.

Stunned, I collapsed on my bunk and listened to the conversations going back and forth over the radio net as various people called in reports of the incident. It soon became evident that the VC had shot down the chopper, using a 51-caliber machine gun. The chopper crashed and everyone was killed. The supply sergeant's luck had run out, and the two happy-go-lucky lieutenants I had talked to just that morning were gone.

The mood was more somber than usual that evening in the bunker as we went through our normal routine. It went unexpressed, but I know that each man realized that he could have been on that chopper when it went down. I was especially moved and shaken by the thought that I would have certainly been killed if events had been just a little different. I had been saved by a gin and tonic. It was ironic that the desire for a cold drink actually saved my life, but it seems that life is like that at times.

I was moved more by this escape than all the other close encounters I had experienced with mortar rounds, rockets, and rifle bullets. That night, I woke up in the middle of the night and couldn't sleep. When I did get back to sleep, I dreamed I saw Death standing at the foot of my bunk in a black hood. I thought again about Dave's words, "Our mothers are praying for us." I was having my third wakeup call.

God was knocking at my door again. He was reminding me that I am mortal, and as a mere man, I needed to be more concerned about my purpose and my soul. I began to believe then, and I firmly believe now, that I had been spared for a reason. I do not think that I was special, or that God had put some hedge of protection around me. I do believe, however, that he has a purpose in mind for each of us, and that my purpose at that time had not yet been fulfilled.

In the middle of the night I prayed the Lord's prayer, as was my custom, but then I added this fervent prayer, "Dear Lord, I do not know if you saved me from this catastrophe today, but if you did, I thank you for it. I know that I can do nothing by my self, and that my strength comes only from you. I will strive to be a better person and to follow your rules. Please accept the souls of the two lieutenants and Sergeant Wallace. This I pray in the name of Jesus my Lord and Savior. Amen."

FAITH IS A CHOICE

During those few months in Vietnam I had experienced a lifetime's worth of emotional trauma. I told a friend recently that if a man, like a cat, has nine lives, I used up most of mine years ago. Many of us who have such experiences, close brushes with accidental death or potentially fatal illnesses, turn to our faith at the time of crisis. Proverbs 1:7 says, "The fear of the Lord is the beginning of wisdom." During times of crises we say, as I did, "Ok Lord, now I believe and I will never abandon you again." But then the crisis passes and some of us revert to our old ways. We go back to our old sins, and we forget Jesus and his teachings and his sacrifice for us. Worst of all we begin to believe the ways of the world and ignore the soft voice of the Spirit. The doubts creep in.

Even Billy Graham, the greatest evangelist of the twentieth century, had his doubts. His biographer, John Pollock, tells us of a time when Billy was wracked with doubt and faced his own crisis of belief. It was in the summer of 1949 when Billy was thirty years old. He had already begun a very successful pulpit ministry and he was president of Northwestern Schools, a liberal arts college and seminary in Minneapolis. His friend and pulpit mate, Charles Templeton, was voicing concerns about the validity of the Bible and challenging Billy about his faith. Templeton would eventually become an avowed atheist, and reject his faith altogether.

Pollock reports that Billy became confused, struggled with his beliefs, and began to question the validity of the Bible. His crisis came to a head one night while attending a conference in the San Bernardino Mountains near Los Angeles. He went out into the forest at night alone to ponder these issues and pray. Graham tells us in his own words, "So I went back and I got my Bible, and I went out in the moonlight. And I got to a stump and put the Bible on the stump, and I knelt down, and I said, 'Oh, God, I cannot prove certain things, I cannot answer some of the questions Chuck is raising and some of the other people are raising, but I accept this Book by faith as the Word of God.'"[1]

Billy did what we must all eventually do. He *chose* to believe. The choice is similar to the one we make in love and marriage. We "fall in love" with a person. For a while, maybe for a long while, we are infatuated with this person, but eventually the infatuation will diminish, and we have to look at the person with sober eyes and ask, "Do I want to live with this person for the rest of my life?" At that point love becomes a choice, not an emotion.

Our faith in God is the same. Every thinking person has doubts at times, but the committed Christian decides that he will believe despite the doubts. The Bible says, "And without faith it is impossible to please God, because anyone who comes to him must believe that he exists and that he rewards those who earnestly seek him" (Hebrews 11:6). If we seek him, he will reward us with faith.

SCIENCE CHALLENGES FAITH

Many people lose their faith when they are confronted with the teachings of science that seem to contradict the teachings of the Bible. Darwinism and scientific theories about the creation of the earth create doubts. Some Christians would ban these scientific teachings all together. Others insist that our schools teach "creationism" alongside the teaching of "Darwinism." Neither of these approaches, in my opinion, will work. Rather the schools should be encouraged to teach what is truly science and fact and at the same time teach what is theory as only theory. We Christians, on the other hand, should teach the truth that we find in the Bible in our churches.

I have personally wrestled mightily with these issues of science verses theology, and reached the conclusion as stated above, that we must believe by faith, not by reason. I have read Lee Strobel's books, *The Case for Faith* and *The Case for Christ*.[2,3] Both books do an excellent job of reconciling the findings of science with the truth in the Bible, and I highly recommend them to those who are struggling with these issues. A couple of years ago I gave a copy of *The Case for Faith* to a friend who had a teenage son who was conflicted with the seeming disconnect between science and Christianity. Two weeks later my friend admitted to me that he had not given the book to his son yet because he was reading it, and it was helping him to overcome his own doubts. Soon after that, my friend died of a second heart attack, and I was glad that Strobel's words had helped carry his soul to the Father.

Another close friend has read both books and still cannot believe, which demonstrates the fact that ultimately it is by choice, not by reason, that we eventually decide to believe or not believe. Ultimately we must receive God into our hearts not our minds. Proverbs 20:5 says, "The purposes of a man's heart are deep waters, but a man of understanding draws them out."

EIGHT

Leadership

...whoever wants to become great among you must be your servant,
and whoever wants to be first must be your slave...

—MATTHEW 20:26

I have known many leaders in my lifetime, the most memorable being three men that I knew during my tour in Vietnam. Two of these are men we would not want to emulate but the third is Captain Red, a superb U.S. Army company commander whom we met previously in chapter 7. All three were very different in their style of leadership, but all three provide valuable information about what makes a good or bad leader. Since we have already met him before, we will start with Captain Red.

CAPTAIN RED

Early in November, a U.S. Army rifle company arrived at Ben Cau and set up camp outside the southern hamlet. The company commander, a tall redheaded captain, came to our bunker and announced that they had been assigned to stay with us awhile and help the locals defend themselves against the VC. As in the previous chapter, I will call the company commander Captain "Red." A tough, no-nonsense officer, educated at the Citadel, he set up two

81-mm mortars in the company street in front of our bunker and made our place his headquarters. He enjoyed cooking on our stove, watching some television with us in the evenings, and occasionally playing pinochle. Since I was without a second in command at the time, it was nice having another officer around.

About the third day he was there, Captain "Red" announced that he could supply materials, cement, and sandbags to build a fort in the southern village, but that the Vietnamese would need to supply some laborers to work with his men. Dai uy Tail arranged a meeting with the chief of the southern village to discuss the matter. This was the only chief who had not come to call when I took over the team.

The meeting was held in Dai uy Tail's bunker. Captain "Red" described his plan, with Dai uy translating for the Chief. The village chief was rather large for a Vietnamese, and I suspected that he might have been part Chinese. He was an older man with white hair. He listened intently and then answered that the plan was good but that the Americans would have to provide some money to pay the laborers who would help dig the moat and create the berm around the fort. Captain "Red" seemed irritated by this request. He said that he had no money to pay the people. The chief then turned to me and asked if I could provide a little money to pay the people. I said that I did not have any funds at my disposal, which was a true statement. Captain "Red" argued that he was supplying the materials and men and expertise and that the Vietnamese could at least provide some labor. The chief shook his head, indicating he did not know what to do.

At this point, I also became a little irritated with the chief, thinking that this was the least they could do. I said to the chief, "Someday we will have to go home. I will no longer be here, and the Americans will not be here to protect you. And then the VC will come. If you are not strong, they will come into the village, and the first thing they will do is kill the chief." I looked squarely at the chief as I said this. He knew it was true. It was such a simple truth, but it was like it had not occurred to him before. He said, "OK." He would find the people somehow. On the appointed day of the construction, there must have been one hundred laborers there, men and women, young and old, digging the moat and packing the earth into a berm. It was finished in one day.

Soon after the arrival of the American rifle company, the enemy gave them, and us, a welcoming salvo of mortars. It was late afternoon when it started. Captain "Red" was in our bunker, cooking a package of freeze-dried shrimp. The mortar rounds began landing in the village and inside our compound with their characteristic sound, a loud but dull thump. We all looked at each other and yelled, "Mortars!"

Captain "Red" immediately ran outside, which didn't seem like the smart thing to do, but I followed. As I stepped outside, I saw "Red" assembling his 81-mm mortar crew. He turned, looked at me, and yelled, "Give me a coordinate, and I'll return fire!"

I ran up to the porch of the headquarters building where our Vietnamese lieutenant was already on his radio, getting the suspected position of the VC mortars. As soon as I got them from the lieutenant, I wrote the coordinates down and called them out to his crew. Then I watched in amazed admiration as "Red" stood there with his crew, shirtless with his hands on his hips, barking out orders as the enemy mortar rounds landed inside our compound. Some were very close, but he never flinched.

After ordering his crew to fire several rounds, he told me to also give the coordinates to his artillery forward observer (FO), who ran over and stood next to me on the porch. The FO was a young first lieutenant artillery officer, who was a little overweight with a slightly pudgy face. He had an olive complexion and dark, curly hair. I will never forget the look on his face. He was terrified. The mortar rounds were also falling near our position on the porch, and there was no cover. The numerous holes in the roof testified to the fact that the VC had long ago determined the coordinates of this building and used it as their favorite target.

The American FO was so nervous that he was shaking all over. He could hardly give the fire mission over his radio. Looking at him made me realize that I had changed. I was still afraid but I had somehow become used to the danger. Soon after the firing started, dead and wounded soldiers were brought in and laid out on the floor. I still felt sympathy for them, but the feeling was not as sharp as before. I had also become accustomed to seeing death and injury. After several rounds were fired from Captain "Red's" mortars, including a salvo from the artillery, the incoming enemy rounds abruptly ceased. I suspect that Charlie learned that day that if he was going to shoot at us again while the Americans were there, he had better be ready to clear out fast.

I have said already that I thought that Captain "Red" was a good company commander. This little introduction to him tells us some of the reasons that he was a good military leader. First he was a man who took his job and his responsibilities seriously. This is a thing called duty in the military. He put duty first. Secondly, he would not compromise his standards because he had a thing called honor. Thirdly, he led from where every good leader must lead, and that is out front.

He was an up-front kind of leader because he came out into the field with his unit instead of staying back at headquarters where he would have been more comfortable. When the shooting started he left the safety of our bunker and personally directed his men in returning fire. He demanded much of his men but he was always there with them. He was the kind of small unit leader who gets the job done and wins wars for our country. There will more about his brand of leadership later but now let's look at another kind of leader who is less effective, but this may not necessarily be his fault.

A YOUNG LIEUTENANT

About three weeks after our return to Ben Cau, I received a call from district headquarters to report with one of my men for a three-day trip to a neighboring village in the southernmost part of the province. Apparently the major had volunteered us to accompany a local Vietnamese company on night ambushes in the area. This company had successfully sprung an ambush two days before, killing two VC, and the Major thought they might repeat the event if we were along.

That afternoon, Mack, Nea, and I climbed aboard a helicopter to take a short ride south to the small village, which was located southwest of Go Dau Ha. When we disembarked at the village, we were led to an American captain, who had also been sent there to conduct joint operations with the Vietnamese. He then introduced me to a young Vietnamese lieutenant in charge of the local Regional Forces. He had set up his headquarters in a rather large, wooden building in the middle of the village.

The captain explained that one of his American lieutenants would take out one of his platoons while I would go with a Vietnamese platoon to ambush outside the village that night. It seemed like a pretty simple plan. We would all hike out into the middle of a large rice paddy nearby, and as the sun went down, we would split up with the Americans going into the woods to the left and our Vietnamese platoon going into the woods to the right. The idea was to arrive at our respective locations just after dark so we could set up our ambushes without being observed by the enemy or their spies.

We knew that enemy spies were prevalent, but we would learn later that afternoon that they were more active than I had previously imagined. The Vietnamese Communists have recently disclosed that their spies were everywhere. They were seemingly common people—children, women, and old men—who paced off distances to our facilities and to important targets within our facilities and gave detailed reports to the enemy. We are now told that Vietnamese barbers were favorite recruits because they learned all kinds of useful information while cutting the hair of the men and officers inside U.S. bases.

Since we had a couple of hours before we had to go out, I sat down on a bunk to rest for a while. After only a few minutes, two young Vietnamese soldiers came in and stood before me, one of them repeating a word that sounded like the Vietnamese word for medicine. I shook my head and said I did not understand.

After a few minutes of not communicating in this fashion, the young man dropped his shorts, revealing that his private parts were terribly infected with venereal disease (VD). I stood up, told the two men to stay where they were, and went outside to find Nea. I told Nea to find the Vietnamese commander and to bring him to me. When they arrived, I told the lieutenant, with Nea translating, that his man was terribly sick with VD and that he must be sent to the hospital in Tay Ninh as soon as possible. The lieutenant agreed and they all left, considerably shortening my rest time before the operation. I never understood why the man came to me first instead of to his commander, unless he thought he wouldn't be treated without my intervention.

At about one hour before dusk, I met with my Vietnamese counterpart and the American lieutenant. I reviewed the operation with them, looking at the map and marking the route and ambush positions with my grease pencil. As we started down the road through the village with our patrols, the American lieutenant walked by my side. He was short and a bit heavy.

"Did they tell you about me?" he asked.

"No," I replied anxiously.

"Well," he said, "this is my first operation."

"You must mean this is your first ambush," I said cautiously.

"No," he said, "This is my first operation. In fact, this is my first day in the field."

"Don't worry," I said. "You'll be OK. Just follow me."

He smiled, looking relieved, and we proceeded on down the road.

Just as we came to the edge of the village, enemy mortar rounds began to fall on our position. We all crouched down at the side of the road, and I observed that we had immediately taken a couple of casualties among the Vietnamese civilians. It was a very uncomfortable feeling to be in the open with little cover to get behind. It was merely a matter of chance whether a round would fall near us or not.

Soon the Vietnamese lieutenant was at my side with coordinates of where he thought the VC were located. I tried to call in an artillery strike on the target on my radio but got no response. The Vietnamese lieutenant grabbed my arm and led me across the road to a small fort where he had a radio set up with a tall antenna. The operator found our frequency, and I was able to call in the fire mission. Soon our artillery was falling in the nearby woods, and the enemy fire ceased. The spies had not only informed the enemy of our time of departure, they also had pinpointed the very moment that we would be approaching the edge of the village. It was not an encouraging introduction to the new American lieutenant on his first day on the job.

When the firing had ceased, we all got up and proceeded to move out again. When we reached the middle of the rice paddy, it was almost dark. I nodded toward the tree line on the left, showing the American lieutenant where he was to take his patrol, and told him we would meet him back at the same spot in the morning. The rice paddy was large, and by the time we hiked across it to the right wood line it was dark.

The Vietnamese lieutenant picked a spot he liked next to a well-traveled path and had his men dig foxholes and set out their claymore mines. He had his men dig foxholes for Mack and me as well as for himself. The ground was soft, and the work went quickly. Before long, we were all settled down in our foxholes with our weapons pointing down the trail.

Soon, a gentle rain began to fall. At first it was a refreshing relief from the heat, but after awhile, the rain became steadier and became quite unpleasant. I was tired, and despite the rain, I fell asleep in the middle of the night. When I awoke, it was raining hard, the night was pitch-black, and I couldn't see two feet in front of me. My foxhole had filled with water up to my waist. It was one of the few times I remember being cold in Vietnam.

I rose out of my foxhole, sat on the edge, and leaned over to talk to Mack. "Hey, Mack," I whispered. "You OK?"

"Wet," he said.

"I know, pretty miserable," I said. "Can you tell what time it is?"

"No, can't see a thing," was his reply.

I told Mack that I would tell the Thieu uy that we should leave right before dawn so that we would get back to the middle of the field by first light. I told Nea, who then told the lieutenant, who agreed, and we all hunkered down for what seemed to be another couple of hours.

Finally, the sky began to lighten a little, we all got up, secured our weapons, and retrieved the claymore mines. It was still fairly dark as we left the woods, but by the time we began weaving our way across the rice paddy dikes toward our rendezvous point, it began to lighten. The rain slackened and was replaced with fog. As we came closer to the middle of the field, I began to see what looked like large, black humps sitting on the dike in the middle. At first they reminded me of a heard of black cows, lying in a field in the rain, but as we drew closer, I realized they were the American patrol. I figured they must have left their position even earlier than we did to beat us back to the middle of the rice paddy.

As I approached the lieutenant, I said, "You must have left really early to get back here before us."

"We never left," he replied. "The men thought they saw some movement in the trees and refused to go any further."

I looked around at these men, and they were the most pitiful looking American soldiers I had ever seen. Of course, they were wet and dirty, but most of all, they were just beat down. There was a look of deep fatigue and despondency about them. There was no spark of life, and they reminded me of large lumps of wet, green moss sitting there in the fog.

That day, and many days since, I have asked myself what I

would have done if I had been that young lieutenant, facing a platoon of rebellious soldiers. I decided that I would have taken my senior NCO and would have scouted out the ambush site. Then I would have returned to tell my men that it was clear and that we were going in. I would have said that any man who didn't go with me would be court-marshaled and that if any man ever refused to obey my order again, he would find himself in the stockade in the morning. I hope I would have done that. I cannot really say, though, because, thankfully, I was never in that position.

This young lieutenant was not necessarily a bad leader. His problem was he was inexperienced and not adequately trained for his position. He seemed to want to do the right thing but he was not what you would call a natural leader, he just did not know what he was expected to do, and was not able to improvise in order to come up with a solution. He failed to accomplish his mission because he lacked basic leadership skills. He was well meaning but ineffective. The next leader we will look at was a thoroughly bad leader in the truest sense of the word.

A VIETNAMESE CAPTAIN

In the middle of November, our team left Ben Cau for good and went to another post at Thai Thong, a small village near Tay Ninh City just a short distance from the 25th Infantry Division base camp. The 25th Infantry was located in a very large fortified post that held a PX and other facilities. There was a small church on the base, and I attended services there at least once. I remember that it was a pretty, little chapel with an open sanctuary that was held up with large, curved, wooden beams. The walls and the beams had numerous holes in them that looked like they had been made by machine-gun rounds, probably from enemy 51-caliber guns.

About this time, Nea was replaced with another interpreter named Liam. Like Nea, Liam was a likable young man who spoke excellent English and would accompany us on each operation. He was smaller than Nea and almost boyish in appearance. I was sorry to see Nea go. He was very young and very immature, but I had grown to like him. He had been with us on the ambush out of Go Dau Ha where he performed well. Also he had become extremely proficient with English, and I remember his telling me one day, that he could understand much more that he heard from Americans than he could speak.

As usual, we spent a couple of days unpacking our gear and getting settled. Dave directed the setup of our new home, which was in a large sandbag bunker about the same size as the one at Ben Cau. The roof was lower, however, and I experienced a problem of hitting my head on the beams supporting the roof inside.

The Vietnamese group commander was a captain, and the second in command was a young second lieutenant. I liked the lieutenant, who reminded me of the young lieutenant at Ben Cau, but I had a bad feeling about the captain based on information I received from Liam. Among other things, Liam told me that the captain ran a brothel near the gate of the 25th Infantry Division base camp that he called the "Car Wash." Like most Vietnamese structures, it was a modest, wooden building, and it had "Car Wash" painted across the front in large letters. As time went on I would find much more to dislike about this Vietnamese officer.

After only a few days at our new assignment, Liam came to me and said that the Vietnamese group commander was inviting the entire team to a dinner he had planned in our honor. The dinner was held at midday as usual because of the lack of electricity and the danger involved in going out at night. We all assembled in a low, tin roofed, clapboard building that served as the local restaurant. All of our people attended, which at that time consisted of Dave, Mack, our new medic, Liam, and me. The Vietnamese contingent consisted of the group commander, his two lieutenants, and an assortment of NCOs.

The meal was good by Vietnamese standards. There was plenty of chicken, duck, green vegetables, rice, and loaves of freshly baked French bread. There was also lots of cold 33 beer to wash it down. We all ate and drank our fill, and everyone seemed to enjoy themselves.

When the meal was over, the captain stood up to make a speech. He spoke for a short time in Vietnamese, which Liam translated for us. He said that he was very glad that we were there. He said he missed very much the two American lieutenants who had been there before, who had been killed when the VC shot down the helicopter. He went on to say that he knew that we would all be great friends. He closed his speech by saying that he wanted us to provide gasoline, which he would sell, and we would all make a lot of money.

As I listened to him, I was able to put together some pieces of a puzzle that had escaped me before. The two American lieutenants he spoke of were the two young men I had ridden with to Tay Ninh that day when the supply chopper went down, killing all aboard. I had missed the return trip because I stayed in the NCO Club to finish my drink. When I did leave Tay Ninh to return to Ben Cau, I rode on a chopper that was delivering a fifty-five-gallon drum of gasoline to this post, apparently to be sold by the Vietnamese captain.

My Vietnamese counterpart was a real operator, an entrepreneur, who had apparently been able to enlist the aid of my deceased predecessors in his scam. He naturally assumed that we would take over their role, which probably involved participating in the ill-gotten revenue and possibly involving complimentary visits to his whorehouse, the "Car Wash." He was operating more like a two-bit godfather than a military commander.

While he was speaking, I noticed that this captain never mentioned anything about why we were supposed to be there, which was to help him fight the war and help provide security for his region. After mulling all this over for a few seconds, I stood up to reply. Speaking through Liam, I said, "We are very happy to be here, and we thank you for this delicious meal. I also hope that we will all be friends, but there will be no gasoline to sell. We will provide only what we need for our own vehicles. We will help you in any way we can to fight the VC." Then I said in Vietnamese, "*Chung ta giet VC,*" which means, "Together we kill the VC."

The captain, who was still standing, frowned at me and said in English, "Yes, kill the VC, but we need gas."

I answered, "There will be no gasoline." Upon hearing this, the captain turned abruptly and walked out of the room. We all stood up and left in silence. As we left the room, I looked at Dave, wondering if I had done the right thing. He was grinning from ear to ear.

I wasn't sure what I was dealing with or how pervasive the corruption was. The captain seemed to be very open about what he was doing and not concerned about being admonished by his superiors. This led me to think that one or more senior officers at province headquarters may have been involved. I resolved to stay away from him if possible, but I was determined not to be intimidated.

About a week later, I received orders to go on a company size operation into War Zone C. I knew this company would be more like a reinforced platoon as far as size was concerned. A full infantry platoon should number about forty men; however, most units were under strength. A platoon for both Americans and Vietnamese was more likely to have about twenty-five to thirty men. A fully complimented rifle company should comprise around 160 men, but in Vietnam at that time we were more likely to field around sixty to eighty men on an operation that was supposed to be company size.

War Zone C comprised all of the area north and west of Tay Ninh City and was predominantly uninhabited and uncultivated except for a couple of small villages and the land immediately surrounding them. By 1969 a large portion of South Vietnam had been abandoned by the peasants because of insecurity and was no longer producing rice. This had caused the country to move from being a major exporter of rice to becoming a major importer of rice. The American government tried to bring in rice grown in the United States, but the Vietnamese people did not like it, preferring rice grown and imported from other Southeast Asian countries.

We had not been assigned an operation since arriving some two weeks earlier, and I had begun to wonder if this Vietnamese unit ever went out. Finally, the orders came over the radio one night. The route we had been assigned was fairly short, and I calculated it would probably take only four or five hours to complete. We were transported by helicopter to a large clearing, which was covered with grass about thirty inches tall. I suspected that this field had once been a rice paddy that had been allowed to over-grow.

Much to my surprise, the Vietnamese captain was leading the operation. I had figured him to be the kind of commander who would stay in camp when the troops went out. Besides, I thought he was probably too busy with his enterprises to spend time out in the field. Perhaps the lack of having gasoline to sell gave him extra time on his hands. Or perhaps he felt compelled to show me that he did spend some of his time trying to fight the VC.

The operation started out fairly well. The company of about eighty men fell into a line as we started across the field. The Vietnamese captain, Dave, Liam, and I walked about nine or ten men back from the point with our radio operators. After crossing the field, we moved into the woods still in a line. As we proceeded down a trail in the forest, I realized this was not typical jungle. The trees were spread apart, and there was sparse underbrush. After awhile, I recognized that the trees were rubber trees and we were walking through an abandoned rubber plantation.

Soon after entering the forest, we came upon a small pond that had been formed by a low dam across the stream. The beauty of this land captured my attention, and I almost forgot we were a combat patrol in the middle of potential enemy territory. As we proceeded down the trail, I suddenly heard a loud explosion behind us. I sensed that the explosion was not normal and involved the spraying of water. Nevertheless, I instinctively dove for the ground as I turned slightly to view the source of the explosion. I immediately realized that one of the men had thrown a hand grenade into the pond in an attempt to kill fish. I sprang back into a standing position and faced the pond. The Vietnamese soldiers broke into laughter as a few small fish floated to the top.

I turned to Liam and said, "Tell the captain that this is very bad, number ten, because if there are VC around, they will know we are here." Liam translated what I said to the captain, who only shrugged and continued up the trail. As we walked through the woods, it occurred to me that we were very vulnerable to ambush. There was basically no point man, and because of the sparse undergrowth, the terrain offered good attack positions from the sides. Also, the ground began to undulate, providing elevated ambush spots where the enemy could pour fire down upon us if they were properly positioned.

I told Liam to tell the captain that we needed to put men out on the flanks and that the point man needed to walk several paces ahead of the rest of the column. The "point" was the most dangerous position on an operation, and it was normal for it to be rotated among the men to spread out the danger. If there were trouble, the point man was most likely to receive the brunt of it, but it was essential to have him out front to avoid leading the whole unit into an ambush. The captain listened to Liam, shrugged again, and continued on without doing what I had suggested.

It became quite apparent that Dai uy was not going to do anything to protect our column of men. I turned to Liam again, and told him in a firm voice that I insisted that Dai uy take the action I had suggested. This time Dai uy stopped and looked at me. Observing the firm expression on my face, he gave orders for one man to go out to each flank and ordered one of the other men to proceed to point. I felt better and continued to be amazed at the natural beauty of the countryside we were traveling through. Since the going was more difficult for the flank men, it was necessary for the whole column to slow down the pace. After awhile, I realized that the flank men had rejoined the column. We had speeded up but were once again exposed to ambush from the sides.

My patience expired. First there had been the irresponsible

throwing of the grenade, and now this pitiful excuse of a commander was trying to lead us all into an ambush with total disregard for the well being of his troops. He was probably anxious to get back to his cathouse and didn't like being slowed down by something as mundane as good security measures.

My job was to advise, not to provide gasoline, so I decided it was time to advise. At the top of my voice I yelled, "Stop!" It worked even though probably half the men didn't know what "stop" meant. They did stop, and everyone turned to stare at me. I turned to Liam, and, still speaking at the top of my voice, said, "Tell Dai uy this is the most screwed up operation I have ever seen!" Liam's mouth fell open. He was speechless. He was afraid to speak these words to a superior Vietnamese officer. "Tell him!" I yelled. "And tell him exactly the way I said it."

Liam spoke in a barely audible voice, but I do believe he repeated what I had said word for word. At this point, he was probably more afraid of me than he was of the captain. When he had finished speaking, I said in a lower but still firm voice, "And tell him that if he doesn't straighten it out, I will make a report when we get back that he will not like." Liam repeated this with a little more ease than the first time.

The Captain gave me a look that could kill. I had done the unforgivable. I had caused him to lose face. I knew it, but I didn't care because I knew that someday these men would be gravely tested, and they would not only lose face, they would lose their lives. The flank men moved back out to their positions without orders, and we completed the operation in strained silence.

I felt sorry for these units under this sorry commander because I knew that someday we Americans would leave and that the VC and their NVA partners would attack, and that these men would have no idea how to defend themselves or carry out a mission. The problem was not with the troops but with the leadership. Their commander was both incompetent and corrupt, a deadly combination. I let my boss, Major Petty, know what I thought. Even though he was supposed to be my counterpart, I don't believe I ever saw this Vietnamese captain again after this operation.

This Vietnamese Captain was most certainly the poorest example of a leader that I have ever experienced. He was only interested in himself and his own selfish enrichment. He displayed no interest in performing his duty to his country or to his men. He had no concept of honor, and no interest in accomplishing his mission as an officer in his country's military. Some military historians have maintained that this type of corruption was a pervasive problem in the South Vietnamese government that extended through all levels from the President's office all the way down to the lowest government officials and through the South Vietnamese military officers corps from the Saigon generals down to local commanders. The captain that I have just described was the only officer that I ever met who was openly and thoroughly corrupt, but his existence tells me that there must have been many more.

ATTRIBUTES OF A GOOD LEADER

Leaders have many styles of leadership, but there are certain principles of leadership that all effective leaders must possess. All people possess strengths and weaknesses, and leaders also have strong suits as well as weaknesses. The key factor that makes a leader successful is that his strengths outweigh his weaknesses. If a leader possesses a good measure of the following qualities, there is a better chance of success:

Duty
In order to lead, a person must be headed somewhere and a good leader must be headed in a direction that others will want to follow. A leader must have a mission, and he must be determined, convicted as my Baptist friends say, to do his duty to accomplish that mission. In his book *The Purpose Driven Life*, Rick Warren tells us that each of us should have a "Life Purpose Statement."[1] In business

we say we should have a "Personal Mission Statement." Whatever you call it, we should each have goals and aspirations that are worthy of emulation, and it is helpful if we take the time to write a "Life Purpose Statement," that we can keep and refer to from time to time. I wrote out my own personal statement several years ago when I studied *The Purpose Driven Life*, and keep it by my desk where I can refer to it easily.

Duty is the personal commitment that a leader has to accomplish his mission in the best way possible. Robert E. Lee, probably the best military leader this nation ever produced, said, "Duty ... is the sublimist word in our language. Do your duty in all things ... You cannot do more—you should never wish to do less."

Character

This is a catchall word for all of those human traits that we admire in people that make us want to follow them. Character includes admirable traits such as integrity, honor, honesty, humility, and generosity. We follow people with character because we feel that we can trust them to do the right thing and take us in the right direction.

Henry and Richard Blackaby have written a book called *Spiritual Leadership*.[2] In chapter 5 they describe several sources of influence people may use to become leaders. First, people can assume leadership because of their position. They may acquire position by being promoted in their company to be managers or officers. Some people are elected to leadership positions in government or other organizations. In the U.S. military, every person is potentially a leader because of his or her positioning in the chain of command. From the Generals on down to the privates, everyone knows his position in the chain, and knows that if the person above him is removed for some reason he must assume that role and take over the duties of the missing leader. There was a young lieutenant in my Infantry Officers Basic Course who had received a battlefield commission in Vietnam. He had been an enlisted man, a platoon sergeant, when during a battle everyone of rank above him in his company was either killed or wounded. He took over as commander of the company. He performed so well that after the battle his commanding General promoted him to Second Lieutenant.

The second way a person can become a leader is through power. This is not usually a method to be admired, and an example would be a dictator who assumes leadership through the exercise of intimidation. Leadership may be seized through power, but it is generally hard to maintain without the leader becoming suspicious and more intimidating towards those around him.

The third way to become a leader is through personality. This method would include performers such as movie stars. Very often this style of leadership is not based on any real ability but is based on the image projected by the person. People who have charisma can exert this kind of leadership, but it seldom has very much durability. When I was at ROTC summer camp there was a young man in our training company that we all liked. He had a winning personality, was funny and entertaining. People tended to follow him around to see what he might do next. When we got our leadership scores from our commander, he did not score well and he said, "I believe that a real leader is someone that people want to follow." I remember thinking, "This may be true, but would I really want to follow this man into combat?" Later I heard a rumor that he was killed by a VC bullet while water skiing in the Mekong Delta. I don't know if this is true, but I have seen his name on the Vietnam Wall in DC.

The fourth and most durable source of leadership is through character. People can soon tell when a leader has character and they will respond positively. Paul calls some of these character traits that we admire the fruit of the Spirit. He says, "But the fruit of the spirit is love, joy, peace, patience, kindness, goodness, faithfulness, gentleness and self control" (Gal 5:22). The best leaders are those who not only display these fruits, but also always strive to be led by the Holy Spirit in everything they do.

One of the most important aspects of good character is humility. David, the ancient king of the Israelites, possessed this quality of humility as well as many other qualities of good leadership. When his deceitful son, Absalom, rebelled against him, King David was forced to flee for his life. He left Jerusalem with all of his household and his most faithful soldiers. As they proceeded down the road into the desert, a man named Shimei came out of his house and cursed David and threw stones at him.

The book of Second Samuel tells us the story in chapter 16:5–14. "Then Abishai, son of Zeuriah said to the king, 'Why should this dead dog curse my lord the king? Let me go over and cut off his head.'" But David told Abishai, "'Leave him alone: let him curse, for the Lord has told him to. It may be that the Lord will see my distress and repay me with good for the cursing I am receiving today.' So David and his men continued along the road while Shimei was going along the hillside opposite him, cursing as he went and throwing stones at him and showering him with dirt." David could have easily silenced this detractor, but he chose instead to try to learn something from the experience. He showed humility in the face of criticism, and he was eventually able to regain power by displaying real leadership through character.

Out Front Leadership

In the beginning of this chapter we got a glimpse of the leadership style of Captain "Red," the commander of the rifle company that was stationed at Ben Cau for a short while. We saw that he was an "out front leader" who left the safety of our bunker during an enemy mortar attack to go outside and return fire with his mortar crew. We also saw the young lieutenant who did not know what to do when his men rebelled. He probably eventually learned that he would have to lead his men into difficult situations in order to gain their confidence. My guess is that he either learned to be an out front leader or that he completely lost control of his platoon.

When I went on my first combat operation at Ben Cau, I accompanied a patrol from a Vietnamese rifle company that was stationed in the neighboring village. The company commander was a Vietnamese first lieutenant who was probably between thirty-five and forty years old, which is quite old for a lieutenant. After a pleasant walk through open country, we eventually entered a small patch of jungle and began walking down a small jungle path. After a short time, one of our men stepped on a trip wire that was attached to a noise devise that had apparently been left there by an American long-range patrol that had spent the previous night in those woods. The Americans had put out the devises to warn them if the enemy was approaching their position. As we moved on, several more of these very noisy devices were set off and everyone became quite nervous, wondering if the next wire might be attached to a mine or booby trap. After awhile I became aware that all of our troops had fallen back behind us and the Lieutenant was walking point. I spoke to him through my interpreter. "The lieutenant should not be walking point." I said, "A soldier should be at point." The lieutenant stopped, turned and looked at me through small wire rimmed glasses. "Sometimes," he said, "a leader must lead."

King David displayed many attributes of excellent leadership, and for the most part he was an out front kind of leader. However there was one instance when he was not a good leader, and the experience brought him much anguish and caused the death of his infant son.

Second Samuel 11:1 tells us, "In the spring, at the time when kings go off to war, David sent Joab out with the king's men and the whole Israelite army." In those days Kings went with their armies into battle, and David had always done so in the past. However, that spring he decided to stay in Jerusalem and failed to do his duty, which was to go with his men. While lounging about in his palace, he noticed the beauty of Bathsheba, began an adulterous relationship with her, and eventually had her husband murdered. As punishment, God took from him his infant son.

There is a lesson here for all of us. Whenever we are tempted to shirk our responsibilities as leaders, we are in danger of falling into situations that will not only cause us trouble but can potentially damage those who have chosen to follow us. People are willing to follow us because of the character traits that we exhibit that give them confidence in our leadership. If we betray any of those principles of good character, then we will fail to lead as God intended for us to lead. If we are always leading from the front, we will be less likely to fall into traps that will detract from our God given missions.

Competence

If we are to be good leaders we must be proficient at whatever tasks we, or our people, will be required to undertake. We need to know our professions well, and we need to be concerned with the details. Douglas Southall Freeman described this quality in Robert E. Lee in his biography of the General. Freeman wrote, "Yet [Lee] had all his life the desire to excel at the task assigned to him. That was the urge alike of conscience, of obligation, of his regard for detail, and of his devotion to thoroughness as the prime constituent of all labor. He never said so in plain words, but he desired everything that he did, whether it was to plan a battle or to greet a visitor, to be as nearly perfect as he could make it."

We each need to prepare ourselves through education, training, and experience. Whenever possible we need to improve our abilities and seize opportunities for service that will prepare us to be better leaders. We have seen how the young American lieutenant did not know what to do when his men rebelled. This was primarily due to a lack of training and experience that he had not yet had the opportunity to acquire. Captain "Red," on the other hand, led with the confidence that came from knowing his profession and being able to impart that knowledge to his men.

God has endowed each of us with different abilities that he wants us to use in his service. Paul says in Romans 12:6 that "We have different gifts, according to the grace given us." However, these abilities must be developed if they are to be used effectively. It is our responsibility as leaders to study our profession or task and to seek as many opportunities for gaining experience as possible.

SPIRITUAL LEADERSHIP

When we speak of methods for effective leadership we naturally think of secular leadership and secular methods. In their book, *Spiritual Leadership*, Henry and Richard Blackaby describe spiritual leaders and give guidance for their development. They note that spiritual leadership is required of those leaders who are directly connected to religious organizations, such as preachers or other church leaders, but they maintain that any leader, whether secular or religious, can and should be a spiritual leader. They say that spiritual leaders must do five things in order to be effective. Spiritual leaders must pray, work hard, communicate, serve, and maintain a positive attitude.

All but two of these activities, prayer and servanthood, may be found in a secular book on leadership. The Blackabys say that prayer is the first and most important thing that an effective spiritual leaders should do, starting each day with prayer, and then continuing to pray during the day as challenges and situations arise. When we are surrendered to God, nothing important should happen or be undertaken that we do not turn over to him in prayer. Mark 1:35 tells us that Jesus started the day with prayer. "Very early in the morning, while it was still dark, Jesus got up, left the house and went off to a solitary place, where he prayed." Some people are not early risers, and we are not commanded to be early risers, but we are commanded to pray. "Watch and pray so that you will not fall into temptation. The spirit is willing, but the body is weak" (Matthew 26:41). And we are told that we will be strengthened through prayer. "The prayer of a righteous man is powerful and effective" (James 5:16b).

Service is the mark of any great leader. It comes from a sense of duty towards and love for their people. The Blakabys tell us that,

"First, servant leadership flows from the love leaders have for their people. Scripture says, 'having loved His own who were in the world, He loved them to the end.'" There have been several news articles and TV reports about soldiers who have been wounded in Iraq. When these wounded warriors are interviewed, they invariably say they want to get back to their units. I am sure that these young people would not use the word, but I believe that they want to return to their units not just because of a sense of duty, but also because they love their comrades in arms. A leader must love his people and be willing to serve them as Jesus did.

NINE

Transition

I have fought the good fight,
I have finished the race,
I have kept the faith.

—2 Timothy 4:7

The day finally came for me to start the journey back to the United States. On the day before my official departure, I took the work chopper into Tay Ninh. Before leaving, I told Mack and Lieutenant Liebhardt good-bye, wished them good luck, and reminded them that they would also be leaving soon. Dave and Mack were both rotating in March. Liebhardt had just arrived in November, and, of course, had a good deal of time left on his tour. Dave volunteered to go with me to headquarters and drive me to Saigon.

At Tay Ninh, we picked up our jeep and headed south down Highway number 22. We stopped along the way at Tra Vo so that I could return a shotgun that the company commander, First Lieutenant An, had lent me. An graciously received its return and expressed his sorrow to see me leave. I also told Lieutenant Man, second in command, and the woman who had cooked our meals good-bye. She cried as though I were one of her own children. It was a bittersweet good-bye. I was extremely excited about going home, but I had grown genuinely fond of the people at Tra Vo, and it was hard to say good-bye.

When Dave and I arrived at Saigon, we went immediately to MACV headquarters where I got my orders and signed up for my flight to the States. My plane would not leave until late the next day, so Dave drove me to the BOQ (Bachelors Officers Quarters) where I would spend the night. Dave helped me carry my gear inside and walked me back to the jeep. "Well, Dave," I said, "This is good-bye," as I extended my hand.

He shook my hand, but replied, "Oh, no, this isn't good-bye. I'll spend the night with some friends and come back to see you off in the morning."

"Sure," I said, "That's a great idea." I watched as he climbed into the jeep and drove away, knowing he would not be back. Somehow I knew Dave was not a man who liked good-byes, and he would not be back in the morning. He was as fine a man as I have ever known.

The BOQ was full of men who were going home. They were happy and loud, and there were card games going on all over the room. Bottles of booze passed freely from bunk to bunk, and nobody slept that night. Thoughts of home conquered any attempt to sleep. Bright and early the next morning I went out to the airport, boarded a large commercial type airplane and returned to the good old United States of America.

When we arrived at the Los Angeles Airport the experience of setting foot on United States soil again is almost impossible to describe. Leaving a war-torn third-world country and returning to the United States with its clean streets, manicured landscaping, tall buildings, and bucolic countryside gave me a feeling of exhilaration I had never known before and have never experienced since.

During a presidential candidates' debate on television, Republican candidates were asked to describe the thing that they would hate to lose the most. I was intrigued by John McCain's answer. He said that the thing that he would hate to lose the most is this country of the United States of America. He said that he lived without his country for several years while he was a prisoner in a North Vietnamese prisoner of war camp, and he would never want to live without it again. I never experienced anything like the hardship that McCain experienced, but I certainly share his sentiment about this country. I also never want to be parted from it again, and have a great appreciation for the immense privilege we all have in being able to live here.

ADJUSTMENT ISSUES

There has been a lot of discussion about Vietnam veterans and their acclimation to civilian life after returning home. Certainly some have not done well, and their misfortune has been broadly publicized in the media. Our local newspaper ran an article about Jessie Jones, Jr., a Marine who had earned the Silver Star in Vietnam, but who recently died in jail.

A section from the article read, "Jones, who was 54, died in March after he fell 20 feet over a railing in the Wake County jail. A decorated Vietnam veteran, Jones fell apart after the war and ended up homeless, sleeping on a cardboard box by an automated teller machine in Boston. A cousin in Raleigh put him up in an apartment, but he often ended up drunk on Poole Road, telling war stories." The article goes on to explain that he fell over the second-story railing while being chased by another inmate with whom he had fought earlier.

The crazed Vietnam veteran is a familiar story we have seen before in the press and in movies, but it is, by far, the exception and not the rule. We have learned that all veterans from all wars have experienced some form of adjustment problems when they return to civilian life. It used to be called "shell shock," or "battle fatigue," but today we call it "post-traumatic stress disorder." Whatever you call it, it's the same thing that any soldier who has seen a lot of combat is likely to experience, but most soldiers adjust and go on living normal lives. Like most returning soldiers, I had disturbing dreams when I returned to the States. At first there were several different dreams, short renditions of things I had seen or done. Soon there was only one dream, which was replayed for me night after night, year after year.

In this dream, I would replay an event that never happened but that I always feared would happen. In the dream, it is night, and I am on the berm of our fort at Ben Cau, looking out into the darkness. A horde of VC begins to rush the fort, firing their weapons, and screaming as they come. I lift my rifle and shoot them. I know that I'm hitting them, but they do not fall. They come right up to me, charging, shooting, and screaming, and then I wake up. This dream became so frequent that I would say to myself in my sleep, "Here it comes again." The dream stopped about ten years ago.

A few years ago, a pleasant theme appeared in my dreams. I am back in Vietnam and there is no war. It's sunny, and I'm walking around a large lake with a Vietnamese lieutenant, who is telling me about the facilities there. It's a pleasant stroll in the sunlight, and the lake is quite beautiful. That dream stopped a couple of years ago, and today, as far as Vietnam is concerned, I am dream free. While doing research for this book, I learned that there actually is a large lake in the northeast section of Tay Ninh Province. If it was there during the war, I was not aware of it. In addition to the dreams, I had what I can only describe as mild, nervous ticks that would occur unexpectedly on some days and would wake me up at night. The other strange phenomena that still affects me occasionally, is that whenever I become frightened of something, I can smell and taste gunpowder.

The wars in Iraq inspired another whole round of dreams. The last dream, which occurred about a year ago, had me standing on some kind of balcony overlooking a courtyard. It is dark and my job seems to be to prevent anyone from crossing the courtyard. I have an M-16 rifle in my hands and as I watch the area below, a man wearing a light blue shirt and khaki pants enters the courtyard from the other side. He is carrying an AK-47 and begins to run toward my position with his rifle at port arms. As he crosses the courtyard I say, "No, stop! Don't do it," but he does, and as he runs toward me I lift my rifle and shoot him several times in the chest. Unlike my old repetitive Vietnam dream, he is obviously hit and falls to his knees. As he falls forward, I see the ragged exit wounds in his back, and he remains frozen in that position until I wake up.

Despite the dreams, the nervous ticks, and occasionally being startled when a truck backfires, I have led a fairly normal life. So far at least, I have not performed any crazed war-inspired acts, not shot up any bars, and not fallen over any second story rails in the county jail. The other Vietnam vets I have known also seem to be living fairly normal, productive lives.

For the most part, the Hollywood portrayal of Vietnam vets as traumatized, war-crazed misfits has perpetuated the lack of respect and honor for these brave warriors. Even now I will occasionally meet someone who, when learning that I served in Vietnam, will say something like, "That's too bad. I hope you weren't too traumatized by it," or "I'm sorry, I hope it wasn't *too* bad." Occasionally I hear a simple, "Thank you," which feels much better. Figuratively speaking, we may have finally learned that it's time to get the Vietnam vets off the "psycho ward" and into the "halls of valor."

POST TRAUMATIC STRESS DISORDER (PTSD)

Jack Epstein and Johnny Miller compiled the available information on PTSD and published it in an article in the San Francisco Chronicle on June 22, 2005. According to the article, PTSD was not officially recognized as a clinical condition until 1980. Prior to that time it was labeled "battle fatigue" or "shell shock." They say that according to the Veterans Administration, one of every twenty World War II Veterans have reported having bad dreams, irritability and flashbacks. In 2004 there were still 25,000 World War II veterans who were receiving disability for PTSD.

There have been no studies of Korean War inspired PTSD, but the authors quote a Korean War researcher as saying that 30 percent of all living Korean War veterans have symptoms of PTSD.

Vietnam is the war that popularized the team PTSD, and the article indicates that 15.2 percent of male veterans and 8.1 percent of female veterans of that war are thought to have the disorder. Of the males, almost half of these have been arrested or spent time in jail. In 2004, 161,000 Vietnam Veterans were still receiving disability compensation for PTSD. Around 30 percent of all Vietnam Veterans report having had symptoms at some time in the past.

The first war in Iraq seems to have had very little effect because of its short duration and limited casualties. The war in Afghanistan is reported to have 18 percent of its veterans displaying symptoms of PTSD, and the second war in Iraq seems to be producing PTSD victims at the rate of one in six. Another related statistic for this modern conflict is that for every one American who is killed in Iraq another seven are wounded. In World War II, there were two wounded for every one killed and in Korea and Vietnam the ratio was three to one. Presumably, the extremely rapid removal of the wounded and the excellent trauma treatment that they are receiving is limiting the number of soldiers who die from their wounds. This statistic also indicates that the carnage is much greater than it seems when one only looks at the number of reported deaths. We can also expect greater instances of psychological problems from these physically wounded vets. Additionally, there seems to be a correlation between the amount of combat a soldier has seen and the chances that he will experience PTSD.

The symptoms of PTSD vary widely among veterans, but the ones most often reported are flashbacks, recurrent images, disturbing dreams or nightmares, anxiety, restlessness, difficulties concentrating, memory loss, irritability, anger, sleeplessness, hyper vigilance, and exaggerated startle response. A related condition is called "survivors guilt," where soldiers feel guilty for having escaped when their comrades were killed or severely wounded. My own experience is that this feeling is widely shared by my fellow veterans even if they have no other symptoms of PTSD.

TREATMENT FOR PTSD

Although I have related having experienced several of the above-mentioned symptoms for some time after returning from the war, I have never received treatment for the disorder. I would count myself among the 30 percent of Vietnam Veterans who have reported having "some symptoms" in the past. There has been, and still is, some perceived stigma associated with admitting this. Soldiers who are still on active duty are particularly reluctant to admit having a problem for fear that it might hurt their advancement in the service. I personally believe that it is not possible for a person, any person, to experience something like mortal combat and not be affected, both positively and negatively, by the experience. The problem comes when the symptoms begin to cause difficulties in the person's functioning in everyday life. Alcoholism, drug abuse, spousal abuse, suicide, social dysfunction, inability to retain employment, and other self-destructive behaviors have all been blamed on this disorder.

The unfortunate marine veteran described in the beginning of this chapter is an extreme example of how this disorder eventually resulted in the death of one of its victims. We have also seen in an earlier chapter how our hero Danny may have been suffering from this malady even before the condition was labeled PTSD. If he continued the way he was headed without treatment, he most likely did poorly in the battle of everyday life once he became a civilian.

The fact that roughly 30 percent of all Vietnam Veterans report having had symptoms sometime in the past, but only half of these people still have PTSD, tells us that some do recover from the malady. Obviously, anyone who is suffering from these symptoms should seek treatment, and the VA purports to stand ready to provide it to all who qualify.

A recent professional article described the forms of treatment that are available.

Janis Kelly published an article in the January 2006 edition of *NeuroPsychiatry Reviews,* entitled "New Approaches Help Heal Combat-Related PTSD."[1] She quotes Dr. Matthew J. Friedman, Executive Director of the V.A.'s National Center for PTSD, as saying, "We now have tested, validated treatment options of PTSD that have been shown to be effective by high standards of evidence-based medicine." He goes on the say that one method is cognitive behavioral therapy (CBT), talk therapy, while the other treatment is with SSRIs (drugs) that have been approved by the Food and Drug Administration for this purpose. He notes that CBT is the most effective but is limited by the number of trained personnel. I personally know two veterans who are undergoing this type of talk therapy in group settings.

Dr. Freeman ends the interview by saying, "The most important factor in whether an acute stress reaction will become chronic PTSD is social support, including support from the soldier's combat unit, family, community, and wider society. Because of the political polarization of the nation during Vietnam, some people took their displeasure out on the troops, young men and women who had risked their lives, when their real anger was directed at decisions made by the country's leaders. Our nation has grown up, and I think we are now sophisticated enough not to confuse our feelings about the war with our feelings about the warrior."

PEACE

It is important for those who have experienced traumatic events such as war to be cognizant of difficulties that they may be experiencing and seek treatment if needed. However, the thing that we all ultimately need and seek is peace. The Bible says, "Do not be anxious about anything, but in everything, by prayer and petition, with thanksgiving, present your requests to God. And the peace of God, which transcends all understanding, will guard your hearts and your minds in Christ Jesus" (Philippians 4:6,7). This is particularly true for those who are suffering from substance abuse. Many veterans are trying to dull their memories with alcohol and drugs. They are trying to use these destructive substances to protect their hearts and minds, when they should be surrendering themselves to God.

In the article mentioned above, Dr. Friedman admits that the therapies he is using are only partially effective. He says, "About 50% of patients with PTSD will achieve complete remission with CBT alone and about 30% with SSRIs alone." The missing ingredient is faith. Paul tells us, "Therefore, since we have been justified through faith, we have peace with God through our Lord Jesus Christ through whom we have gained access by faith into this grace in which we now stand. And we rejoice in the hope of the glory of God. Not only so, but we also rejoice in our sufferings, because we know that suffering produces perseverance; perseverance, character; and character, hope. And hope does not disappoint us, because God has poured out his love into our hearts by the Holy Spirit, whom he has given us" (Romans 5:1–5).

Those who are suffering from the trauma of war, as well as those who feel that they are losing the battles of life, need the peace of Christ who said, "I have told you these things so that in me you may have peace. In this world you will have trouble. But take heart! I have overcome the world" (John 16:33). None of us have the strength to totally win this battle on our own. "When a man's ways are pleasing to the Lord, he makes even his enemies live at peace with him" (Proverbs 16:7). Where can we go to find this peace with God?

THE CHURCH

The Church is not a building. It is not even an organization. It is the body of people, which Paul calls "the saints," who have come together with Christ at their head for the purpose of worshiping and communing with their God. "And he is the head of the body, the church" (Colossians 1:18a).

Despite the objections that some people have to organized religion, I believe the church is the still the best place to learn about God as revealed to us by Jesus. It is also the best place to seek emotional healing and to find brotherhood and sisterhood among people who share their beliefs and are dedicated to a better way. "He came and preached peace to you who were far away and peace to those who were near. For through him we both have access to the Father by one Spirit. Consequently, you are no longer foreigners and aliens, but fellow citizens with God's people and members of God's household, built on the foundation of the apostles and prophets, with Christ Jesus himself as the Chief cornerstone" (Ephesians 2:17–20).

Many people today are receiving their spiritual inspiration from Christian ministries over the television. There is nothing wrong with this, but unfortunately there is a very strong movement of TV preachers who seem more concerned with creating their own wealth, than they are with saving souls. Some of these preachers wear fancy clothes, drive expensive cars and travel in private jets. They try to convince people to send them money by preaching that whatever they give will be returned to them several fold. It is true that God wants us to support our church and help those less fortunate, be we are probably wiser to give to our local church and through proven legitimate international aid organizations. There are many horror stories about people of little means borrowing from their credit cards in order to send money to these charlatans so that they can buy more silk ties and vacation houses. I firmly believe that there is no substitution for a local church that is backed by a denomination or other legitimate organization.

It does not matter much what church denomination you chose, as long as it is a church that is Bible based in its teaching. It is also best if your church is dedicated to serving its entire people and making a difference through service in its community. The preacher in your church should also be a pastor, who is a shepherd, to his people. I once met a man while attending a seminar at the Billy Graham Training Center in Asheville, NC, who is responsible for recruiting preachers for an evangelical denomination in the South Eastern United States. When I asked him to define the most difficult part of his job, he responded that the hardest thing for him was to find pastors who are shepherds. He said, "I find lots of people who want to be preachers, but not many who really have a heart to be shepherds."

TEN

Winning the Battle of Life

You have made known to me the path of life,

—PSALM 16:11

When I left the war and returned to the United States in February 1970, I returned to a life that seemed to have taken on new meaning. My life then seemed charmed and fantastic. I had an appreciation for my home and homeland that I had never known before. I arrived in Virginia on the eve of an ice storm that covered the landscape and made it into a crystal wonderland where the trees glistened and even mundane objects, such as trashcans, were transformed into things of beauty, their shabbiness hidden by the ice. I spent hours the day after the storm walking through this wonderland, soaking in the cool beauty, wiping from my mind the hot and dusty images of Vietnam and the war.

During those first days at home, I spent some time indulging in the things I had always loved. I spent a week at my Uncle's farm in the rolling hills around Gordonsville, Virginia. I went quail hunting with my cousin Robert and my brother David, and when we found a covey of birds, the dog pointed, and we walked past him to flush the quail in a thunderous rise of flapping wings, I was so mesmerized by the experience that I forgot to shoot.

Everything seemed better than I had remembered. The old farmhouse that had been built by my grandfather now seemed to be a structure fit for a picture postcard with its white clapboard siding and its structural simplicity. The farmland had become a place of breathtaking beauty with its green pastures and wooded creek bottoms. I seemed to notice for the first time that the Blue Ridge Mountains on the western horizon created a picturesque backdrop to the farm, its rustic barns, stables, and out buildings.

As I traveled around Virginia, becoming reacquainted with the people I had known, they seemed to have taken on new personas, some seeming to have become wise, while others were now sophisticated, or smart, or beautiful, or cute, or funny, or sage. Others, who before had been just ordinary, were now extraordinary. Rednecks had become rustic philosophers and bearers of wise pontifications. I viewed my friends, my immediate family, and my relatives in a new light. They were now all wonderful people, worthy of admiration and love. My father, it seemed, had made the greatest transformation. He had turned from a dull man with stodgy unreal ideas about life into a wise man, imbued with practical knowledge and sage advice.

During those early weeks at home from the war, I would awake each morning with a feeling of thankfulness, eagerly jumping out of bed at dawn exclaiming out loud, "Thank God! I'm home! I'm alive!" After my wife and others in the house explained that they were also happy about my return, but they would prefer I express it at a lower decibel so early in the morning, I continued to be thankful but in a quieter voice.

Following those first couple of weeks, I started a course of graduate study at the University of Richmond. I was delighted to be back in an academic environment, and approached my professors with a new appreciation for their wisdom and knowledge. I was eager to prepare for my new civilian career and attended to my studies with an enthusiasm to learn that far exceeded what I had known in undergraduate school.

Some of these feelings of appreciation for our homeland and its people have lasted until today, but naturally most of them have faded over time. I realize now that the people and places had not changed at all. I had changed, not them. The experience of war and living in a third-world country had given me an abiding appreciation for this nation and our way of life, but I soon realized that my life could not go on being just a series of new highs and new exciting revelations.

Since those early days after the war I have experienced much. I have seen successes and failures. On the failure side, I have experienced the devastating pain of divorce and seen its negative effects on everyone concerned. I have seen success in business come and go, and I have seen commercial ventures end in failure. I have moved about, making and losing close friends in the process, and I have seen both of my parents die. On the positive side I have experienced remarriage to a beautiful Godly woman and received the privilege of getting to know and love her children. I have seen my business recover and prosper. I have experienced the comfort of knowing that my deceased parents now rest in the loving arms of the Lord. And I have found a loving community of believing brothers and sisters. Life is a continuing battle that goes on as long as we live, a battle that is comprised of advances and retreats, victories and defeats. Life is a battle.

THE BATTLE

"Why does it have to be so hard?" she asks. "My grandson has autism, and my son and his wife are struggling to deal with the disease, but the doctors say there is no cure, and it just seems so hopeless. Why has God allowed this to happen to them?" The speaker is a woman in her late sixties, well educated and intelligent. She is asking me this question because we are in an adult Sunday school class and I am the teacher. I have heard the question before, framed in different circumstances, but still the same. As always, I struggle to give an answer. I want to say, "How should I know? I am probably the worst sinner in the room. God has not given me any special knowledge. He has merely thrust me into this chair at the front of the room and said, do your best with what you have." Having struggled with this question for many years, I give her the best answer I can.

This question is very important. It has caused a number of people to lose their faith. Charles Templeton, former evangelist and friend of Billy Graham, cited it as the major issue that caused him to become an atheist. In an interview he told Lee Strobel that he lost his faith when he saw a picture of a starving African woman on the cover of life magazine. The magazine said that she was living in an area of extreme drought. Templeton noted that all she needed was a little rain, and he couldn't understand why a loving God didn't give it to her when it was God who was supposed to be in charge of the rain. Templeton just could not believe in a God who would allow such a thing to happen.

The general question is why does a good and loving God allow so many bad things to happen? The answer I have derived from my reading and study is based on the concept of "free will." God has given us free will to make decisions for ourselves and to order our lives in whatever ways that we choose. He has created a world for us to live in that is wondrous but in some ways dangerous. He gives us the right to choose to love him, to love and respect our neighbors, and to live righteous lives. He also allows us to make mistakes, to choose unwisely, and to bring on harm to ourselves and to others. If he were to intervene each time we confront any sort of calamity or illness, would we really have free will or would we be more like puppets on a stage?

One might say, "Ok, I agree with the free will thing, but why does the world have to be a dangerous place? Why can't it be harmless so that everyone would be safe?" If that were the case then our choices would be limited. If the forces of gravity were arrested when I decided to jump off the top of a tall building, then I would no longer have the free will to choose to harm myself. "But why," one might ask, "does there have to be disease?" That is like saying why should there be tigers in the jungle since they are dangerous and if you run into one on a jungle trail he might eat you. Should we ask God to do away with the tiger portion of his creation at the same time that we ask him to do away with the disease microbe portion of his creation? Should we ask God to change any of his creation or change any of his laws of nature? God asked Job, "Do you know the laws of the heavens? Can you set up God's dominion over the earth?" (Job 38:33). It is not our job to tell God what portions of his creation we do not like.

One problem with this concept of free will is that it leaves too much up to chance, and there seems to be no real need for God. If we stop at this point in the argument, life seems to be one great roulette wheel, where a spin of fortune may land us in front of a tiger or on top of a polio germ or in a rose garden. Undeniably, good things and bad things do seem to happen in a random fashion, but it is necessary for us to also consider the will of God and the power of prayer as they relate to these events.

I do not know why my men and I were saved from certain death in the rice paddy that night next to the river. Did God stop the machine gunner at just the right moment or did he just get tired of firing? Did God answer my prayer? I believe that he did because he willed it and he listened because I was willing to surrender my will to his. Why doesn't he always save us? If he did then there would be no consequences and no free will. He intervenes when it serves his purpose. Like Job, we cannot always know his purpose, but we must trust in him nevertheless. Our trust must be like that of my friend Yogi Yarborough, who knew he was dying, but still trusted in God and his provision for his servant. "'For I know the plans I have for you,'" declares the Lord, 'plans to prosper you and not to harm you, plans to give you hope and a future'" (Jeremiah 29:11).

Life is a battle because it is dangerous and because as human beings we are all destined to struggle. The battle is for many things. Naturally we must struggle for the physical things we need: food, housing, employment, and health care being the primary necessities. There is also a battle raging for the emotional things we need such as human relationships, respect, self worth, love, and creativity. Finally, there is a battle raging for our hearts, and this battle may be the hardest of all since the foe is found in the spiritual realm as well as inside each of us. For us to be successful, the battle must be joined on all fronts.

TO GAIN YOUR LIFE YOU MUST LOSE IT

I carry in my pocket a key ring that has a small pendant attached to it that is in the shape of a nail. One side of the pendant is flat and "Gal. 2:20" is written across the flat surface. Galatians 2:20 reads, "I have been crucified with Christ and I no longer live, but Christ lives in me. The life I live in the body, I live by faith in the Son of God, who loved me and gave himself for me." I received the pendant four or five years ago at a Promise Keepers Conference in Raleigh. When it was given to me, I immediately picked up my Bible and read the verse, but I did not understand it.

From time to time I have reread this verse still not fully understanding it until recently when I read a book by John Piper entitled *Don't Waste Your Life.* Piper refers to this verse and says, "When Christ died, we died. The glorious meaning of the death of Christ is that when he died, all those who are his died in him. The death that he died for us all becomes our death when we are united to Christ by faith."[1] He goes on to explain that when we accept Christ and surrender ourselves to God our old self dies and our new self takes over. In effect, the old self dies with the crucifixion and the new self rises with the resurrection. Mark 8:35 says, "For whoever wants to save his life will lose it, but whoever loses his life for me and for the gospel will save it."

In the third episode of the HBO series "Band of Brothers," Private Blithe admits to Lieutenant Spears that he was seized with fear on the day of the invasion of Normandy and never left a ditch where he was hiding. In an attempt to give Blithe some encouragement, Spears offers him this rather perplexing bit of advice, "Blithe, the only hope you have is to accept the fact that you are already dead. The sooner you accept that, the sooner you'll be able to function as a soldier is supposed to function." The Lieutenant is not speaking biblically but he still helps to make the point. We all must accept the fact that we will eventually die someday, and if we agree to die now to our old self and begin to live as our new self, we will begin to have the courage and the power that we need in order to succeed in the battle of life.

Jesus explains this condition as being born again. In John 3:3 he tells Nicodemus "I tell you the truth, no one can see the kingdom of God unless he is born again." Many Christians have heard this phrase so many times that it may seem a bit shop worn, but it is truth. Just as we must die with Christ we must also be born again with Christ.

I have heard a number of Christians give their testimony of their conversion, and many will report this experience as akin to being struck by lightning. John Wesley, on the other hand reported his experience at a prayer meeting as a feeling of "being strangely warmed." That was certainly not a lightning bolt experience, but it was still significant for a man who would go on to establish the Methodist Church. For some of us, particularly those raised in the Church, the experience is more gradual. I have talked in this book about personally receiving three "wake-up calls" to accept the Christian life, and I must admit that it is a process that continues to this very day. Regardless of whether it is gradual or sudden, we must all reach a point where we are willing to give up our old self and take on a new life in Christ.

KNOWLEDGE AND SPIRIT

To continue to win the battle, we must continually grow in knowledge and spirit. We do this in two ways. First we must read and study the Bible. Some say that they cannot do this because the Bible is too hard to understand. The truths of the Bible are actually very simple. The Old Testament is the story of God working on the earth through his chosen people, the Jews. The story is told over and over again in different ways, but it is the same story. The New Testament is the story of God acting again on the earth, but this time by sending his son with a new message. The message is that God is love, and mercy, and grace. The story is told in different ways, but the massage is the same.

It is not enough to just know the basic message. We must learn all the different aspects of the message, just as we get to know all the characteristics of a friend or spouse. We grow spiritually by reading and studying the Bible, and we should do it each day. There are several daily devotionals that can help. The one that I use and recommend is Henry Blackaby's *Experiencing God Day-By-Day*. I am now on the third reading of this book and find that it is a great way to start the day.[2] The second way that we grow spiritually is through prayer. Just as we should read the Bible daily, we should also pray daily as discussed in chapter 8. These prayers don't have to be long. They can be short little petitions or praises. When our prayers are petitions, we should always remember to add "thy will be done." You can be assured that your prayers will be answered. The answer will not always be what you expect, but Psalm 37:4 tells us "Delight yourself in the Lord and he will give you the desires of your heart."

God wants us to talk with him just as any parent wants to hear from his children. Whenever I used to call my parents in the last years of their lives, my mother would always end the conversation by saying, "You have made our day!" This let me know how important my call was to them, and reminded me that I should do it again soon. God is like that. He wants us to check in occasionally. As we wage our daily battles, it is good to check with The Father to gauge our progress.

THE GREAT COMMANDMENT AND
THE GREAT COMMISSION

Before Jesus departed from this earth, he gave his disciples, and us, two charges that are important challenges for us in this battle called life. These charges, which are sometimes called the two Cs, are the Great Commandment and the Great Commission. We find the Great commandment in Matthew 22:37 where Jesus said, "Love the Lord your God with all your heart and with all your soul and with all your mind. This is the first and greatest commandment. And the second is like it: Love your neighbor as yourself." We are therefore commanded to love God and to love our neighbor. Where do we find these neighbors that we are supposed to love? We find them everywhere. Of course, we find them next door, but we also find them on the street, in the work place, in stores and shops, in restaurants, on the highway, and anywhere else we may go.

We especially find the people that we are supposed to love among our Christian brothers and sisters. A friend of mine recently said, "I have discovered that what really matters in this world are relationships." Because I know that my friend is a Christian, I know that he means Christian relationships. The best place to make those kinds of relationships is in the church. Jesus also said "A new command I give you: Love one another. As I have loved you, so you must love one another. By this all men will know that you are my disciples, if you love one another."

The other people that we are supposed to love are those who

are not believers and some of these may be far away. This brings us to the Great Commission, which was given to us by Jesus in his last words to the disciples. "Therefore go and make disciples of all nations, baptizing them in the name of the Father and of the Son and of the Holy Spirit, and teaching them to obey everything I have commanded you. And surely I am with you always, to the very end of the age" (Matthew 28:19,20). This commandment has been appropriately called the marching orders for Christians.

We tend to think of foreign missions when we think of this commission, but there is much fertile ground of mission work all around us. All of the places listed above as to where we find our neighbors, are the same places where we might practice this commission to spread the gospel. We spread the word in two ways. First we do it through our actions as we live the Christian life. People observe us and make opinions about Christianity by the way they see us act and by the way they hear us interact with other people. The second way we can spread the gospel is through direct testimony to others about the saving grace of our Lord. We must be very careful about how we do this. We must be bold enough to broach the subject, but not so brash as to offend and turn off the listener.

The work place is the ideal spot to practice this commission. I belong to an organization called CBMC (Christian Businessmen's Connection). It is a group of men, primarily businessmen, who are dedicated to bringing the good news of the gospel to the work place. The idea is to spread the word from one man to one man at a time in his place of work. The organization is made up of teams of men that are located in most cities in the United States and in some foreign countries. I belong to a small CBMC team that meets each Wednesday morning for one hour at 6:30 a.m. for prayer and a little Bible study over coffee. Meeting with these men has been a wonderful experience for me for a couple of reasons. It gives me a chance each week to meet with other Christian men who love the Lord and are dedicated to their churches and their families. Also, they are men I can trust to provide good advice when I need it, and to serve as a reminder if I ever begin to stray from my rightful course.

Foreign mission work is also something that is within the reach of many of us, and we don't have to give up our day jobs. My church, and many other churches, sponsor short foreign mission trips, one to two weeks, at reasonable cost to the participants. My wife and I have gone on a couple of these trips, and have found them to be beneficial to ourselves as well as to the people with which we have visited. In Vietnam we worked in a hospital for a week, while last year we helped to build a new church in Lima, Peru. The people in these countries are much more impressed with the work of volunteers than they are with the efforts of paid workers, and they know that we are Christians.

CHRISTIAN SOLDIERS

There is an old hymn that I used to love to sing entitled "Onward, Christian Soldiers." The first line of the hymn is, "Onward, Christian soldiers! Marching as to war, with the cross of Jesus going on before. Christ, the royal master, leads against the foe; forward into battle, see his banners go!" It can be found on page 575 of the Methodist hymnal, but during the late 1970's and early 1980's there was strong pressure to have it removed because it was thought by some to be "too militaristic." Fortunately, it was retained by the Hymnal Revision Committee when the hymnal was revised in 1989, but I have not heard it sung in a church in many years.

For me, this hymn symbolizes the spirit that is needed today in the Christian community. People need to be inspired and emboldened to take up the cause of Christ, and there is a great need today for more Christian soldiers. They are needed in our military, in each branch of the Armed Services. The military needs more soldiers, NCOs, and officers, who are willing to demonstrate that they are people of Christian character, who support and live lives that reflect

Christian values. This can be done primarily through example without violating any military regulations against proselytizing.

Just as there is still a need today for soldiers to protect our country and defend our way of life, we also have a great need today for civilian Christian soldiers in the battle of life. There is a need for more prayer warriors, warrior missionaries, warrior pastors, and warriors for God in the work place. This Christian army needs to be larger, and the skirmish lines need to be long and filled with men and women who are strong and courageous. We may even find a few new recruits who are willing to join our ranks because they are encouraged by the verses of an old hymn to pick up their banners and march "with the cross of Jesus going on before."

Notes

CHAPTER 1
1. Janis Joplin, "Mercedes Benz," Columbia Records, 1971.
2. Henry T. Blakaby, *Experiencing God: How to Live the Full Adventure of Knowing and Doing the Will of God* (B & H Publishing Group, 1998).
3. Stu Weber, *Tender Warrior: Every Man's Purpose, Every Woman's Dream, Every Child's Hope* (Waterbrook Press, 2006).
4. Henry T. Blackaby, *Experiencing God: How to Live the Full Adventure of Knowing and Doing the Will of God* (B & H Publishing Group, 1998).

CHAPTER 2
1. Stephen Mansfield, *The Faith of the American Soldier* (Strang Communications Company, 2005), 95–96.
2. John C. Loving, *Combat Advisor: How America Won the War and Lost the Peace in Vietnam* (iUniverse, Inc., 2006).

CHAPTER 3
1. Chris Hedges, *Losing Moses on the Freeway: The 10 Commandments in America* (Simon and Schuster Adult Publishing Group, 2005).
2. Blackaby, Henry T. *Experiencing God Day-by-Day: A Devotional* (B & H Group, Oct. 1998), 15.

3. U.S. Catholic Bishops, "The Challenge of Peace: God's Promise and Our Response" (1983), 18–19.
4. Peter S. S. Temes, *The Just War: An American Reflection on the Morality of War in our Time* (Dee, Ivan R. Publisher, 2003).
5. Ibid., 166.
6. Ibid., 167.
7. Ibid., 168.
8. Ibid., 169.
9. Ibid., 171.
10. Ibid., 175.

CHAPTER 7
1. John Pollock, *The Billy Graham Story* (Zondervan, 2003), 44
2. Lee Strobel, *The Case for Faith* (Zondervan, 2000).
3. Lee Strobel, *The Case for Christ* (Zondervan, 1998).

CHAPTER 8
1. Rick Warren, *The Purpose Driven Life: What on Earth Am I Here For?* (Zondervan, 2002).
2. Richard Blackaby and Henry T. Blackaby, *Spiritual Leadership: Moving People Toward God's Agenda* (B & H Publishing Group, 2001).

CHAPTER 9
1. Janis Kelly, "New Approaches Help Heal Combat-related PTSD," *NeuroPsychiatry Review* (January 2006): 1–2.

CHAPTER 10
1. John Piper, *Don't Waste Your Life* (Crossway Books, 2003), 55.
2. Henry T. Blackaby, *Experiencing God Day-By-Day: A Devotional* (B & H Publishing Group, 1998).